CAROLINA DAY SCHOOL
1345 HENDERSONVILLE ROAD
ASHEVILLE, NC 28803

W9-CQW-022

INVENTIVE TEACHING

THE HEART OF THE SMALL SCHOOL

a revised and expanded edition of

The Teacher as Inventor

Judith S. Kleinfeld

G. Williamson McDiarmid

William H. Parrett

Judith S. Kleinfeld is a professor of psychology at the University of Alaska Fairbanks.

G. Williamson McDiarmid is an associate professor of education at Michigan State University.

William H. Parrett is a professor of education at the University of Alaska Fairbanks.

Cover photo by James H. Barker. Janine Lombardi, a science, health, and physical education teacher from Nenana City Schools teaches a life science ecology project "Population Hunt" to seventh-graders July Blair and Clifford Big Joe.

© 1992 by the College of Rural Alaska, University of Alaska Fairbanks. All rights reserved. Published 1992
Printed in the United States of America

Elmer E. Rasmuson Library Cataloging in Publication Data

Kleinfeld, Judith.
  Inventive teaching: the heart of the small school / Judith S. Kleinfeld, G. Williamson McDiarmid, William H. Parrett.— Fairbanks: Center for Cross-Cultural Studies, University of Alaska Fairbanks, 1992
    p.   cm.
  Rev. ed. of: The teacher as inventor: making small high schools work.
    ISBN   1-877962-22-8
    1. Rural schools—Alaska.   2. Education, Rural—Alaska. 3. Eskimos—Alaska—Education.   4. Indians of North America—Alaska—Education.   I. McDiarmid, G. Williamson.   II. Parrett, William.   III. University of Alaska Fairbanks. Center for Cross-Cultural Studies.   IV. Title
LB   1567.K53   1992

Acknowledgments

Inventive Teaching: The Heart of the Small School has originated from the efforts of many, many individuals. Based on the original *Teacher as Inventor* (Kleinfeld, McDiarmid & Parrett), this revised and expanded version has been created because of the overwhelming popularity of its predecessor. *Teacher as Inventor* was actually spawned from a research project entitled the Alaska Small High School Study, the first comprehensive review of the successes and achievement of Alaska's recently created network of small rural high schools. During the course of that project, the authors (Kleinfeld, McDiarmid, and Hagstrom) discovered a wealth of innovative teachers, schools, and practices, which prompted the creation of *Teacher as Inventor.*

Many thanks are indeed appropriate to the originators of that first effort, including professors Judith Kleinfeld, G. Williamson McDiarmid and David Hagstrom, and research assistants Kathy Lieich, Steve Marble, Charlie Luehmann, Annemarie Kuhn, and Susanna Gascoine. Also contributing to that first effort were Robert Silverman, administrator for special projects at the Alaska Department of Education; Phil Brady, teacher at Russian Mission; and Jim Alter, NEA Alaska.

The creation of *Inventive Teaching: The Heart of the Small School* would have never occurred without the superlative professional assistance, editing, and creative efforts of the directors of the Center for Cross-Cultural Studies Publication Office Barbara Tabbert and Sue Mitchell, with layout and design assistance from Kim Hagen, Rae Ammons Jones, and Paula Elmes who successfully transported this book from rough draft to final copy. Additional thanks go to Zhang

iii

Yixin for the countless hours of telephone and written confirmations, Renee Blahuta for wonderful assistance in the location and selection of photographs, Julie Harrison for early manuscript typing and Ann Dehner for her editorial pen. We are also grateful to Gerald Mohatt, Dean of the College of Rural Alaska and director of the Center for Cross-Cultural Studies that funded much of this effort. We thank Lisa Brosseau and the many other graduate students of the University of Alaska Fairbanks whose comments, assistance in locating photographs and program information, and encouragements have helped make this second version possible.

Finally, we sincerely thank and dedicate this book to the many Alaskan teachers in rural and small schools whose ideas, creations, inventions and successes make this book possible. This is your book!

Contents

Chapter 3: Broaden Students' Experience With Travel Programs

PART II:
TAKE ADVANTAGE OF STATE AND NATIONAL PROGRAMS

Chapter 4: Academic Enrichment Programs:

Chapter 5: Interdisciplinary Programs

Chapter 6: Correspondence Study Programs

Chapter 7: Practical Skills Programs

Chapter 8: Summer Programs

Chapter 9: Social Programs

PART III:
SOURCES OF INFORMATION

Preface

In the course of studying small schools, we discovered instance after instance of teachers using their imaginations to tailor educational programs to the needs of the students. Community members, teachers, and administrators urged us to collect information on these programs and make it available to teachers. We agreed, and in 1986 we first published *The Teacher as Inventor*. After several reprintings, we decided it was time to update, revise, and create *Inventive Teaching: the Heart of the Small School*.

This new version again is directed at teachers who choose to work in all types of small schools. However, it has been most pleasing to note considerable interest and praise for the first book came from teachers and professionals in larger urban settings. After over a century of widespread disdain for the efficacy of small schools; of rampant, often indiscriminate consolidation; and of chronic underfunding, educators have noticed that many small and rural schools have not only persevered, but thrived. A few have achieved magical success.

In a time of deep criticism of our public schools, failed reform efforts, and frequent calls for major restructuring, the small schools of Alaska and their inventive staff welcome inquiry and interest.

In what follows, we start with you, the individual teacher in a small school classroom. You and your classroom are the core. Then we work out from the center—to the school as a whole, to the community, and then to the region, state, and nation. As we go, we will highlight programs and ideas that have been devised to take advantage both of small classrooms and of other resources in the local environment, programs which demonstrate the inventiveness and imagination of teachers at small schools.

Much of what you will find in the following pages reflects straight forward, good teaching practice which indeed has far wider application than the schools of Alaska.

It is our intention that this book be a stimulating resource for you—a collection of ideas and proven strategies that will help you improve the quality of your classroom and your school. We hope these ideas will inspire you.

Making Changes in Small Schools:
The Wheels of Bureaucracy Are Small and Turn Faster

Small rural schools not only can work—they are working. Throughout the United States, teachers are working with community members to find ways to use the strengths and to overcome the limitations of small schools.

In the small western Alaska community of Russian Mission, there were 58 students in the school, 17 at the high-school level, and six certified teachers. In this situation, typically, two teachers would divide the secondary instructional responsibilities. One would teach math and science while the other handled language arts and social studies.

Pat Evanson-Brady, former principal, wasn't happy with the typical arrangement. She asked herself, "Why limit student access to two teachers? Why not use my entire staff?"

With the support of the local school committee, she hired teachers with different academic concentrations. The teachers then taught their specialty to all students in grades two through twelve. For example, rather than each elementary teacher instructing their pupils in math and a secondary teacher teaching algebra and geometry, one teacher taught all mathematics to all students.

The principal's innovation cost no more than the typical staffing arrangement. Students scored higher on achievement tests and enjoyed having a variety of teachers. Teachers felt less pressure and more satisfaction teaching in their fields of expertise.

The new staffing plan lent itself to block scheduling for the afternoon classes. Students had larger chunks of time for integrated projects in journalism and cultural heritage. Local experts taught skin-sewing. Students even started a community bakery from which they learned bookkeeping and planning skills.

Pat relishes the flexibility and opportunities that small schools present. "Never again will I have the opportunity to create a school that I have right now. It is possible to do many things quickly in rural Alaska. The wheels of our bureaucracies are smaller and often turn faster than they might in larger places."

Small Rural Schools are Opportunities for Educational Excellence

Small schools have become an endangered species in the United States. Claiming that small schools are inefficient and ineffective, policy makers throughout the country have been consolidating small schools for decades.

But comprehensive schools, plagued by discipline and morale problems and watered-down curricula, have not lived up to their billing. Teacher initiative and concern for student learning are often undermined by bureaucratic inertia and the sheer number of students.

Educators throughout the country are rethinking the issue of small versus large schools. Many districts have initiated small alternative schools or created a small "unit house system" in large, impersonal schools.

Small schools may be limited in the academic and extracurricular programs they can offer. Teachers frequently teach outside their fields in multigrade classrooms. These problems are more than offset, however, by advantages such as the following:

- *Low student-teacher ratios.* Teachers have time to tutor, to go over student work carefully, and to monitor student progress closely.

- *The chance to get to know students and their families.* In small communities, teachers can spend time outside of school with their students and their families. They often become adopted members of the large extended family that many villages are.

- *The opportunity to significantly influence the lives of students.* Teachers are critical members of many communities and are important role models for young people.

- *Relative freedom from burdensome bureaucracy.* Teachers often have a latitude for their ideas and actions that is the envy of their urban counterparts.

- *Economies of scale.* Planning an American heritage trip for a student body of 17 is manageable whereas such a trip for 1,700 students is unthinkable.

How Do You View Small Schools?

Teachers who view small schools as opportunities to tailor instruction and curriculum to local needs and resources are a prime ingredient of schools that are exciting places for students and staff alike.

Frequently in education our view of what is possible is shaped by our past experience as students. Our image of school is often that of the large comprehensive schools many of us attended. Consequently, we may inappropriately impose our image of much larger schools, an image formed under circumstances usually quite different from those in rural Alaska, on the small village schools.

Small schools cannot be comprehensive. They lack the diversity of teachers, pupils, and courses as well as the extracurricular activities. At the same time, these schools have a wealth of advantages that make them among the most promising educational opportunities to be found anywhere.

A Cautionary Tale: Don't Blow Up the Well

While Pat Evanson-Brady's story illustrates teacher inventiveness in seizing the opportunities that smallness presents, veteran teachers warn newcomers about making changes too quickly or without careful regard for the consequences.

In Saul Bellow's novel, *Henderson, the Rain King*, Henderson wished to do something good to demonstrate his affection for his adopted African village. Finding that the villagers wouldn't use the local well because of an infestation of frogs, he dynamited the well. He got rid of the frogs but destroyed the village water supply at the same time.

Lest you blow up the well in your efforts to demonstrate your good will and affection, heed the advice of veteran teachers in small schools:

- Go slow.
- Let people get to know you first and become comfortable with you.
- Establish trust.
- Be cautious in making judgements and arriving at conclusions.
- Expect that people will not respond as you might wish.
- Expect disappointments.

A Final Disclaimer

We have made every effort to verify the information in this book. We have interviewed teachers by telephone to assure that we have described programs and projects accurately. In many cases, we have used the exact wording from brochures supplied to us. We have mailed drafts of our descriptions for review to the teachers responsible for the program or idea and to the resources and agencies represented.

Despite these efforts, we expect that we may have inadvertently erred in describing some of the programs. Agencies change and information gets outdated. We take responsibility and apologize in advance for such errors.

Where possible, we have provided addresses. We encourage you to contact program offices directly for additional information. Many times the specific teachers named in the book have moved on. Nonetheless, we mention them by name and the community in which they worked because we want to give them recognition for their educational inventions.

Several of the programs and strategies are no longer operating. We continue to list them because they are good ideas and do work—they just may be enduring a temporary hiatus due to a teacher leaving, funding cuts, or myriad other reasons.

It is, of course, impossible to publish a complete listing of all the resources available to teachers. We have tried to present a selection of organizations, programs, and available resources in this book. We encourage teachers to join the professional organizations that best represent their area of interest and subject matter speciality. Receiving the journals of those organizations is the best way to become aware of and involved in numerous opportunities and available resources in any particular area.

For us, the bottom line is that teaching in small schools is a rare opportunity to make a real difference in pupils' lives and to have fun doing it. We hope this book contributes in some small way to your making a difference—and to having fun.

PART I

WORKING CLOSE TO HOME

Draw From All the Resources in Your School

Doing It Yourself

To make a small school work, you need to use imagination. In this chapter, we show what rural teachers are doing with

- their own talents,
- the school staff,
- the students,
- technology, and
- scheduling.

■ Your Most Valuable Resource Is Your Own Talent

Tutorials

Research and common sense both underscore the powerful effects of one-to-one instruction on student learning. Benjamin Bloom's research "The 2 Sigma Problem: The Search for One-to-One Tutoring" *Educational Research* June/July 1984 has shown that small tutorials result in higher levels of participation and interaction, closer monitoring of student learning, greater task engagement, more higher-order thinking, and far greater achievement.

Small schools have an enormous advantage over large schools in that the small school lends itself to tutorial instruction. Teachers can plan instruction to maximize their one-to-one work with students—as Liz Simpson did for 15 years in Nulato.

Nulato Master Teacher Liz Simpson Tutoring a Student

"Tony, did you ever find the information you needed for your report on mountain climbing?"

Leaning both arms on the table, Liz looks at the boy through her glasses.

"Not yet." Tony is fingering his dog-eared papers like a rosary.

"Right, now," Liz says, "get me the 'M' encyclopedia so I can show you what you need to do."

Liz opens the encyclopedia. "Look under 'Mountaineering.' You want some information on the people who climb mountains."

Liz scans the room, picks up some unauthorized activity on her radar, and deals with it. She turns back to Tony, "Get a clean sheet of paper."

Liz starts to demonstrate taking notes, talking Tony through it. "Never copy word for word. So I'll just put down the information: 'Between 1921 and 1958, eleven expeditions . . .'" Pointing to the encyclopedia open before her, she continues, "Now,

ALASKA WRITING PROJECT

you're going to take this same information and put it in your own words. Then, you want to read a little bit more."

How To

Tutorials offer an excellent opportunity for modeling and guided practice:

1. *Demonstrate the skill.* Model the skill you are trying to teach. Talk the student through what you are doing and explain exactly why you are doing it.

2. *Don't leave out steps.* Experienced teachers, because they are experts, often skip over steps that novices need to work through.

3. *Watch the student practice the skill.* After you have solved a math problem, for example, have the student solve the identical problem. Then watch the student solve a similar problem.

4. *Give immediate feedback.* Don't let errors become bad habits. Help the student right away.

The Multisubject Class

"Third period. Let's see, that means I'm teaching typing. And accounting. And photography. Hmmm . . . What am I going to do? I'll just put them all together."

Darla Chevalier, business education teacher in Tanana, was undaunted by the prospect of teaching three different subjects to six students in one period. Teachers come to expect such arrangements in rural schools. Why complain? After all, Kim Mason taught beginning and advanced typing, bookkeeping, and business management in the same classroom in Alakanak. Bill Radtke, the wizard of the multi-discipline classroom, juggled math, social studies, creative writing, and typing during his first period class—before his first cup of coffee!

Imagine spinning from one subject to the next: Amidst a spirited explanation of *Macbeth*, a call from the algebra students forces you to thrust the bloody knife from your mind. As factorials come into focus, you're called to elucidate the moral philosophy of the Declaration of Independence. Turning, turning in the widening gyre, the teacher cannot tell factor from factotum! How do the Darlas, Kims, and Bills of the world do it? This is what they told us.

How To

1. *Consider student needs and interests in deciding which courses to combine into one class.* You may develop your own curriculum for the courses or you may wish to order correspondence courses (see Correspondence Programs).

2. *Schedule your multidiscipline class to coincide with your physical and psychological peak.*

3. *Organize materials and resources for each course in advance so students won't outpace you.* Organization will enable you to focus your attention and energy on instruction.

4. *Prepare a folder for each student.* The folder should contain the course objectives, a list of resources, and a schedule of assignments and due dates. Hand out the folders on the first day and explain their contents.

5. *Keep units short.* Five to ten days is a good range.

6. *Give students a schedule of assignments each week.* This plan should be clear enough so students know exactly what they should be doing each day. Special projects should be included for students who finish sooner than anticipated.

7. *Establish a routine for working with each group or individual.* Providing students with a signal—a flag or other indicator—that they can use to indicate they need assistance will prevent students having to wait in line for your attention. In the intervals between your regularly scheduled sessions with each group, you can circulate to deal with individual questions or problems.

8. *Use peer tutoring.* Designate a student in each course to whom others can go for help (see Peer and Cross-Age Tutoring).

9. *At the end of each period, update each student folder.* Check off completed assignments and adjust scheduled assignments to individual students' progress.

10. *For multilevel classes in the same subject matter, occasional introductory lectures or reviews for the whole group may be appropriate.*

11. *After class, sit motionless in a dark room.* Allow Lady Macbeth and Jefferson to sink, hand-in-hand, into the dark recesses of your mind. Let the quiet wash over you. Feeling a little vertigo is OK—after all, you've just been spun.

Variations

- *The Multiage Class:* Recognizing that "grade levels are an artificial method of chopping up a kid's academic development," Dr. Vince Barry at Newhalen places students according to their competence in the subject rather than to their age. A seventh grader may be in a sixth-grade English class one period and a ninth-grade math class the next.

  Determining a student's skill or knowledge level is critical to correct placement. In Newhalen, the staff consults with various itinerant experts to determine student competence. Achievement and diagnostic tests can also be used.

Additional Sources:

Northwest Regional Educational Library
101 SW Main Street, Suite 500
Portland, Oregon 97204
(503) 275-9500

The Project-Centered Class

Project-centered curriculum is an idea with a long educational history. Teachers are well aware of the educational advantages of projects—doing something of real life importance, working in cooperative groups, and having a satisfying product at the end. In large schools, class projects are hard to do. The logistical problems of coordinating different teacher and student schedules, getting out of the school building, and getting out of the 50-minute period often defeat such efforts.

Small schools, on the other hand, readily lend themselves to projects as Eliot Wigginton has demonstrated at the Rabun Gap-Nacoochee School in Georgia. The series of Foxfire books that Wigginton and his students have produced over the years illustrate the project approach at its best.

We need not, however, go so far afield to find examples of curriculum around a series of projects. Look at the curriculum Terry McCarthy taught one year in Newtok. He took students to nearby Mekoryuk for the reindeer roundup.

Students participated in pre- and post-visit activities as well as activities in Mekoryuk. Terry talked about the theme of the project, reindeer herding, as "the thread that tied the whole curriculum together." The table opposite illustrates the different curriculum areas and the project activities associated with each:

Such projects develop many skills critical to academic success: listening, speaking, writing, reading, research, higher-order thinking, and organizing ideas and activities.

Just as important, students derive a sense of accomplishment and pride from the products of their activities. At the same time, the community sees tangible evidence of student learning in the

Subject or Class	Curriculum Thread
Graphics	A photographic essay of the herd and corral
English	Interview essays and personal experiences
Industrial Arts	Building a stretching rack for the hides
Native Arts	Fleshing, cleaning and tanning hides
Science	Anatomy, feeding habits, and animal functions
Home Economics	Instruction in proper meat cuts, wrapping, and freezing techniques
Mathematics	Determining weights, pricing, cost per pound, and trip cost
Alaska History	History of reindeer herding in Alaska

videotapes, newspaper articles, subsistence items, and photographic exhibitions that students produce.

How To

1. *Involve students in choosing a theme for the project and in planning.* This involvement will ensure that students "own" the project and will be motivated for the hard work ahead. Local aides, elders, and others in the community should be involved as well.

2. *Identify the products of the project.* Will students design projects for an audience, produce a video, a book, a magazine or newspaper, or other tangible products?

3. *Clear the project with parents, the local school committee, and others important in the community.* Many a well-conceived project has run afoul of local values. For example, one social studies teacher decided to have her students carry out a survey of subsistence food consumption in the community. Community members perceived the project as a sly attempt to gather data for the Fish and Game Department. As a result, not only did the project fail but the

teacher lost the trust of the village. Involving local aides in the planning process is one way of avoiding problems. Another is to get the permission of the local school committee before beginning.

4. *Coordinate project objectives with the curricular objectives of the school and/or district.* Terry McCarthy and his staff sat down with the district curriculum guides and fitted the project objectives to those suggested for language arts, social studies, science, math, Native studies, vocational education, special education, and home economics. This coordination ensures that students are learning skills and knowledge they will need and that the learning objectives of the project are clearly stated.

5. *Be prepared to restructure the daily school schedule to fit activities.* Terry and his staff found they needed to adopt a "block" schedule with two-hour periods in the morning to carry out project activities that did not fit into the conventional 50-minute periods.

6. *Look around you.* Small schools and small communities lend themselves especially well to project-centered curriculum. Terry and his staff did another project on housing. They used a construction project in the village as an opportunity for students to study traditional shelter, contemporary building techniques, the governmental contracting process, and local hire policy. Many teachers have had students conduct local history projects, organize museums, study local wildlife—the list is almost endless.

Remember the observation: "You may never again have the flexibility in curriculum and instruction that you have in small schools." Have fun!

Variations

- *Vocational English:* Hydaburg students worked on drafting, welding, carpentry, and stove building projects—and then wrote about their experiences in English class. As former Principal Richard Gigo explained, "They have something that they are interested in to write about."

SAM WINCH

During shop, Monday through Thursday, students worked on their projects and wrote draft narratives about what they were doing. In English class on Friday, they revised their drafts and turned them in to be graded.

Students kept journals and step-by-step descriptions of their projects. They also wrote letters to vocational schools, introducing themselves and asking for information.

This idea worked so well in Hydaburg that science teachers expanded their curriculum to incorporate English assignments in science projects.

THE TEACHER AS COUNSELOR

When Dorian Ross became principal of the Togiak School, he brought with him the experience of having started counseling programs in Iran and in Craig, Alaska. In this program, individual teachers serve as mentors for small groups of students.

Here's how his counseling period worked: Dorian explained that the program can serve two primary purposes. Because full-time counselors are an almost unheard-of luxury in small schools, the teacher-counselor can provide career and educational guidance and social and emotional support. Secondly, the program strengthens relationships between the student and teacher. The teacher-counselor acts as scholastic leader, trusted friend, parental stand-in, and adult model. The warmth of the relationships created through the program radiates throughout the school.

How To

1. *"Don't set rules and then expect the students to buy into them,"* advised Dorian. Consult with teachers, students, and their parents.

2. *Creating counseling groups.* At least two approaches may be used in forming groups. One approach is to group students by grade level. This approach has the advantage of familiarity. The students know all the others in their grade. A second approach allows students to choose their advisor. In this approach, students name their first two or three choices. Then the principal apportions students accordingly. This method allows cross-age relationships to develop among the students and is more like the family structure in the community. If you choose the family grouping method, students should be limited to two or three changes of advisors during their six years in junior and senior high school.

3. *Be flexible.* Be prepared to alter the daily schedule to take advantage of unexpected visiting talent such as an archaeologist or visiting doctor.

4. *Follow the morning group meetings with a "cooling out" activity.* For schools using traditional 50-minute periods, a 20-minute block of silent sustained reading works well. With a program structured into the regular school day, teachers have the time and opportunity, often denied by the sheer busyness of schools, to keep up with what is going on with students.

Variations

- *Site Counselors.* Some school districts use teachers as counselors. The site counselors receive assistance, guidance, and direction from the professional itinerant counseling staff of the district. The itinerant counseling staff provide advice, materials, and training to the site counselors as they travel throughout the district. In addition, site counselors are annually brought into the district office for training.

Adequate training, open communications, well-defined roles, and caring staff are the keys to a successful site counselor program.

- *Career Counseling:* The lack of rural school counselors has led some teachers to devise special courses to prepare students to enter careers or postsecondary education. Dina Thain at Klawock has done just that. In Thain's career class, college-bound students hone their study skills while vocational education students practice skills such as résumé writing. Dina says that, since the class began in 1982, "about 60 to 70 percent of the students are in productive fields, doing something for themselves."

Dina has her students establish goals for themselves at the beginning of the year. She shows film strips or holds audioconferences with people in various fields to inform students of the realities of different professions or trades.

Students focus their career interests through self-esteem projects that help them clarify their priorities and identify their strengths and weaknesses. Students also keep journals in which they record their dreams, aspirations, and autobiographical information. Finally, they keep career notebooks in which they record goals and values, job descriptions, their résumé, college descriptions, application forms, and other practical information.

INDIVIDUALIZED STUDY

For some students the traditional classroom is not a place of learning and enlightenment. Instead the classroom is a place where students feel uncomfortable and alienated and lack the skills necessary for success. For many village teachers, these

CHARLES MASON

students appear all too frequently and teachers are sometimes at a loss in determining the best way to help these students learn.

One result of educational research in dealing with this dilemma has been the creation of individualized programs or independent study programs. These programs are centered around the individual student. The student has some say in the manner in which they will study and also in what classes and courses they will take in certain time frames. Students are still required to complete the standard curriculum, but the manner in which they do so is different.

Sources of Information

Research for Better Schools, Inc.
444 N Third Avenue
Philadelphia, Pennsylvania 19123
(215) 574-9300

This organization has developed and disseminated some of the best-known materials and programs for individualization. Materials include Individualized Science (IS), Systematic Progress in Reading and Literature (SPIRAL), Individualized Prescribed Instruction (IPI) Mathematics,

Individualized Middle Mathematics (IMM), IPI Reading, and IPI Spelling.

> Duluth Public Schools
> "The Duluth Plan"
> Attn: Instruction Office
> 215 N First Avenue E
> Duluth, Minnesota 55802
> (218) 723-4150

Duluth public schools have developed individualized programs at the elementary and secondary levels. Emphasis is on involving students in the learning process, both in terms of prescribing work for themselves and in evaluating their work. Contracts are used as the primary means of prescription.

Other Sources

> *Independent Study* (David W. Beggs, ed.)

A collection of readings concerned with independent study practices that have stood the test of time, this book deals primarily with the nature and goals of independent study and ways schools can organize for implementing an independent study program. Published in Bloomington by Indiana University Press, 1965.

> *Education by Appointment: New Approaches to Independent Study* (B. Frank Brown)

This book describes a number of strategies for implementing an independent study program in any type of school situation. It includes a brief but complete history of independent study, an analysis of the need for such programs, and an impressive argument for them. Published in West Nyack, New York, by Parker Publishing Co., 1968.

■ Use the Total Staff

Many of Alaska's small high schools are administratively combined with the local junior high and elementary programs. This creates a rare opportunity to take advantage of the skills and talents of all the teachers in the school system. Below, we describe ways in which rural educators have used the total school staff to increase the quality of schooling.

We have already described Pat Evanson-Brady's assignment of teaching responsibility to her six-teacher staff. Teachers taught their specialities rather than specific grade levels. Phil Brady, Pat's husband, for example, spent his mornings teaching language arts and reading to grades six, seven, and eight. In the afternoon, he taught language arts to the high-school students.

In Koyukuk, two teachers, one certified in elementary education and the other in math and science, were responsible for students in kindergarten through tenth grade. With a background in social studies and training in the Alaska Writing Project, the elementary teacher assumed responsibility for all social studies and language arts courses. Her colleague taught all math and science.

Teachers derive satisfaction from teaching subjects in which they feel well prepared and in which they are interested. They also like the variety represented by teaching all levels. The students have contact with a broader range of adults. They are exposed to a broader range of teaching styles, perspectives, and personalities.

Just as diversity in a gene pool strengthens a species, so departmentalization, by diversifying the pool of talent and knowledge to which students are exposed, strengthens students' educational experience.

How To

1. *Departmentalization starts with the principal.* The principals of the elementary and high schools must plan for departmentalization. They must determine the academic needs of the program and, in cooperation with the district administration and school board, hire teachers and assign them accordingly.

CAL WHITE

2. *Teachers working in departmentalized schools need to consult with each other.* If you are a secondary teacher, consult with teachers who have taught elementary students on methods, classroom management and organization, disciplinary techniques, learning objective, appropriate expectations, and so forth. Because elementary teachers will be teaching high-school students, they may wish to ask secondary teachers similar questions.

Consider subscribing to a couple of periodicals that present elementary school teaching methods. If the school won't subscribe, remember that professional journals are tax deductible.

Variations

- *Using Elementary Teachers in the High School:* Another version of departmentalization involves using elementary teachers to teach their areas of specialization at the high-school level. For example, an elementary teacher with a background in art may teach the high-school art classes. To free up the teacher, either the class is scheduled after the school day ends in the elementary school or the high-school teacher takes over the elementary class.

■ Students Can Teach Students

Peer and Cross-Age Tutoring

In the multigrade, multi-ability classroom typical of rural Alaska, teachers—darting from one student to another, from one subject to another, and from one ability level to another—often wish they could clone themselves. Teachers at the Frank A. Degnan School in Unalakleet have managed to do just that, but with a peer tutoring program rather than with genetic engineering.

The program matches students carefully. Sometimes an academically gifted child learns sign language and teaches sign language to a hearing-impaired child. Sometimes an older student with a learning disability is the perfect choice to teach a younger child with the same disability.

Teachers write out a list of specific learning tasks for the tutor to work on with his or her pupil (such as learning the *a* sound). This record-keeping system lets teachers know exactly how each tutor and student are progressing and where the trouble spots are. When a tutor is having trouble teaching a skill, a teacher can step right in and figure out something new to try.

In small schools, older students teaching the younger ones and advanced students tutoring their peers has a long history. Research shows that such instruction is educationally effective and cost-efficient. In rural Alaska, cross-age and peer tutoring are naturals.

Although Lynn Ontiveros, former resource teacher at Frank A. Degnan School, developed her program specifically for special students and gifted students in kindergarten through twelfth grade, the organizational structure is applicable in other settings. This approach provides training for the tutors, establishes criteria for the performance of both student and tutor, and documents the progress of both.

How To

1. *Choose tutors carefully and match them with younger students.* In choosing tutors, a critical criterion is the potential tutors' communication skills. After the initial training, tutors should be tested to ensure that they can clearly explain the subject matter. Bright students who can't explain clearly may only befuddle their classmates.

   In matching tutors and students, pay attention to personalities and aptitude. Bright tutors who lack patience should not be matched with slow learners. Such tutors are better matched with bright students at a lower grade level.

   Students who have low self-esteem and believe themselves incapable of learning may be best matched with upbeat tutors who inspire confidence.

2. *Train tutors.* Several group meetings with your tutors will allow you to discuss their roles and responsibilities. Specifically, you should address the following:

   Tutors as models: Emphasize to your tutors that they should model not only academic skills and knowledge but appropriate behavior as well. They need to be on time to tutoring sessions, have materials ready so time is not wasted, and put away all materials at the end of the session.

Tutors as teachers: Point out to the tutors appropriate teaching behaviors. These include being aware of any physical, emotional, or social problems that might affect their students' performances as well as monitoring the students' reactions to the lesson. Are they fidgety, bored, lost? Talk about nonverbal indications of student attention such as wandering eyes, frowns, drumming fingers, etc.

Another topic to discuss with tutors is their attitudes. If the tutors are bored or tired, they will communicate that mood to the students and blow any chance of being effective. Point out the importance of being enthusiastic and supportive.

Instructional techniques: Demonstrate to the tutors how to prepare materials, how to find effective exercises, how to ask questions, how to use examples or analogies, etc.

Teach a sample lesson to the tutors as you wish them to teach their students. As you teach, explain what you are doing and why. You may want to pair up the tutors and have them practice tutoring each other as you monitor them. You and the tutors' partners may want to give the tutors feedback on their techniques.

Discuss the use of behavior modification techniques for dealing with inappropriate behavior. Ignoring off-task behavior, positively reinforcing appropriate behavior, and using tokens and points are all techniques that tutors can learn and use.

Tutors will also need instruction on how to correct their students' work and record their performances.

3. *Monitor the tutors.* In addition to observing individual tutors regularly and checking the records they keep on their students, meet with the whole group once a month or so to discuss common problems, questions, and tutoring techniques.

You may also want to have the students evaluate their tutors. Information from an informal survey could enable you to help the tutors adjust their speed, modify their techniques, or select more appropriate materials. Consider using a written evaluation—students are more apt to be critical on paper than in an interview with the teacher.

4. *Give the tutors feedback.* At the end of the quarter, acknowledge your tutors with certificates of achievement presented at an awards ceremony. Give a party for tutors and students to celebrate their hard work.

Peer Counseling

Inspired by the work of the National Chemical People, students at Bartlett High School in Tyonek organized a "Chemical People" town meeting. A panel of six respected and concerned adults in the community discussed their own experiences and served as resources for students who needed help with alcohol and drugs.

Impressed with this effort, students decided to organize a similar group within the school. From an original group of nine peer counselors, the program grew to fifteen students the following year.

Peer counseling not only supplements the meager counseling services available through the school but also reaches students who might not otherwise seek help. For some troubled youth, peers are less intimidating than adults. This seems particularly true for young people with serious problems of substance addiction or emotional depression.

While the success of the program depends on the genuine concern of the peer counselors, a carefully structured program with adequate training for the counselors increases its effectiveness.

How To

1. *Students must want such a program.* To achieve the student ownership needed for the program to succeed, students must be involved in planning and structuring the program.

2. *Selecting peer counselors*. Students who are setting up the program should solicit volunteers. Volunteers should be screened according to a set of criteria such as sincerity in wanting to help others, reliability, positive attitude (including their willingness to work on their own problems), respect for the dignity of others and the confidentiality of all communications, and high standing in the eyes of other students.

3. *Train peer counselors*. Counselors should be taught how to deal with major social problems such as suicide, depression, apathy, substance abuse, and physical and sexual abuse. The following organizations can provide training: The Anchorage Crisis Center, Anchorage Mental Health, Akeela House, RuralCAP, the Inside/Outside Prison Program, and Cook Inlet Native Association's Alcohol Prevention Program. In addition, the health corporation in your region might also provide training.

4. *Develop guidelines:*

- Always have a supervisor in the building in which the conference between the peer counselor and his client is being held.

- All communications are confidential. Counselors can breach that confidentiality only in a life-threatening situation such as a potential suicide or child abuse.

- Counselees may choose their counselors. Post the names of counselors in several places around the school and in the school and village newsletter. Students may make appointments either directly with the counselors or through the school counselor.

- Avoid a prearranged schedule of counseling sessions. Counselors and clients should arrange their own session—outside of class.

- If a counselor must miss a session, he should arrange for another counselor to substitute for him or reschedule the session.

- Counselors should listen noncritically to their clients and be patient. The client is likely to be in a behavioral rut. Despite the rationality and lucidity of the counselor's advice, the client will probably continue to make the same mistakes for some time. For serious problems, counselors should suggest that the client contact a professional organization or ask their client if they can speak to the school, village, or district counselor.

5. *Monitor the counselors.* Meet with the counselors once a month to provide further training and to discuss problems or issues that have arisen.

6. *Additional resources.* The following publications provide more information:

Samuels, Mimi & Dan. *The Complete Handbook of Peer Counseling.* Fiesta Publishing, 1515 NW Seventh Street, Miami, Florida 33125. (Because this was published in 1975, you may have to search for this classic!)

Hannaford, M. J. *Counselors Under Construction.* Pettit Publications, Trumbull Drive, Atlanta, Georgia 30338. 1040. ("One of the best, most upbeat, contemporary books I've read"—Pat Chitty, Bartlett counselor.)

■ **Technology Can Expand Your Power**

Students in the Inupiaq studies class at Ambler High School wrote a series of stories through the eyes of a teenager living in Ambler long ago. They drafted, revised, and published the stories using a word processing program.

Students at Newhalen produced camera-ready copy for their school newspaper and yearbook with a word processing program, a spelling checker, and a page layout program. They wrote their articles and headlines on computer—just like professional journalists.

A Port Lions junior wrote a BASIC program to monitor water conditions in an 80-gallon fish tank containing salmon eggs. Each day he entered the ammonia nitrogen level, oxygen level, and water temperature. The program displays a warning and suggests corrective actions if water conditions approach the tolerance levels of the salmon eggs.

Frontier environments stimulate new ideas and new ways of doing things. Rural Alaska education is a classic case. Alaska's rural teachers are pioneers who are making serious and imaginative use of the new technology available for educators. With the increased use of computers in the classroom, Alaskan teachers are finding the use of telecommunications increasingly more important in staying on the cutting edge of modern education. Telecommunications is based on the ability that computers have to talk with each other using standard telephone lines and modems.

In this section we discuss what rural teachers have been doing with:

- Computers
- Audioconferencing
- Instructional Television
- Video Technology

COMPUTERS

Many teachers who first come to Alaska villages are surprised to see how many computers their schools have. Many rural schools have one computer for every four or five students.

Outside observers are sometimes struck by the apparent contradiction when they see students from remote, traditional villages using advanced computer technology. But computer programs are as at home in rural education as Yup'ik language programs. Students enjoy the new technology. Teachers enjoy the opportunity to individualize instruction and to teach through projects that yield products of professional quality such as a community newspaper.

Many teachers have used the eight Individualized Study by Technology (IST) courses produced by the Department of Education. Others have acquired commercially available software.

Some districts, for instance Yukon/Koyukuk, have developed their own software, carefully tailored to the specific language problems of the students in their district. Their "Alaska Writing Machine" is a word processor that is structured to encourage extensive writing across the content areas.

Computers have the most benefit when teachers go beyond drill and practice programs. Rural teachers are showing students how to use the computer as a tool for (1) writing and revising, (2) storing and retrieving information, (3) making complex calculations, (4) simulating complex situations, and (5) communicating across distances.

How To and Contact

Alaska educators using computers can link up to important support services. We describe them briefly below:

•Alaska Association for Computers in Education

Alaska Association for Computers in Education (AACED) is the professional association for educators who use computers. It sponsors a newsletter, a major conference each year, and a number of contests and information exchanges. Membership is $15 per year. For a membership application write to: Computer Education Specialist, Department of Education, Box F, Juneau, Alaska 99811-0500.

•Alaska Computer Consortium

This consortium of school districts was organized during the summer of 1986 to provide low-cost software, training, software find-and-evaluation services, and general support to educators in participating districts. The consortium distributes Minnesota Educational Computing (MECC) software and operates the Educational Computing Center in Anchorage. For more information, contact: Alaska Computer Consortium, University of Alaska Anchorage, School of Education, 3211 Providence Drive, Anchorage, Alaska 99508.

•Alaska Department of Education

The Department of Education provides technical assistance to school districts in computer education, instructional television, audioconferencing, and distance education technologies.

CHARLES MASON

The department sponsors projects and publications targeting the use of computers to enhance instruction in academic disciplines. Publications available include:

- *Hand In Hand: The Writing Process and the Microcomputer*
- *Writing, Reading, and Reflecting: Teachers and Children Learn Together*

The department is piloting the use of laptop computers and telecommunications in instruction of distance education courses in its Centralized Correspondence Study unit. Students communicate with each other and with teachers using the University of Alaska Computer Network electronic mail system.

Contact

Office of Basic Education
Alaska Department of Education
Box F
Juneau, Alaska 99811
(907) 465-2644

Other Resources

Computers have become closely identified with the process approach to writing instruction. A teacher who has received writing process training will be able to make more effective use of computers in the classroom. Excellent training is available through the Alaska State Writing Consortium. Contact your district's teacher representative or Office of Basic Education, Department of Education, Box F, Juneau, Alaska 99811.

The University of Alaska and postsecondary institutions across Alaska provide many courses in the field of educational computing. The University of Alaska Southeast offers a master's program in educational technology. Contact the nearest college extension center, community college, or university campus for information about course offerings.

Subscribe to one or more of the major educational computing magazines. These are full of information and ideas about using computers in the classroom. Most contain timely software evaluations. The International Society for Technology in Education (ISTE), for example, publishes a monthly journal that keeps classroom teachers informed of opportunities and ideas in computers and related technology. Contact ISTE through the University of Oregon, 1787 Agate Street, Eugene, Oregon 97403-9905.

Math, science, and computer educators have access to computer bulletin boards and electronic communication in their teaching and specialty areas, thanks to additions to ENEWS, the Alaska Department of Education electronic news and information network.

Access to the bulletin boards and to general education information on the main ENEWS bulletin board is easy. Any person with a computer, a modem, and telecommunications software can simply dial up the local telephone number for the University of Alaska Computer Network or Tymnet. Readers need not have their own user IDs. The Department of Education pays for bulletin board usage.

When the system asks "Destination?" type "acad*." When the system asks "User name?" type "RMENEWS" (do not use your regular UACN ID). The next thing to appear on your screen will be the main menu of ENEWS.

From there, it's order up whatever you'd like—news from Alaska Science or math teachers associations; calendars of math, science, or computer events; updates on educational technology; news from the Northwest Association of Marine Educators or the Alaska Natural Resources and Outdoor Education Association; and much more.

Variations

- Students in Unalakleet Elementary Schools have not only integrated their computer knowledge and expertise with other subjects but they are also using computers to send their work to students in Wisconsin. The students have modernized the traditional pen pal letter into a distance-delivered view of Unalakleet through the use of modems and computers. For more information contact Unalakleet Elementary School, Box 225, Unalakleet, Alaska 99684.

- Centralized Correspondence Study, a school administered by the Alaska Department of Education, sponsors three electronic mail newswires. These weekly collections of articles are written by participants who are students or teachers from schools throughout Alaska with University of Alaska Computer Network (UACN) access. Three newswires are available: *Kidbits* for third through sixth graders, *Logjam* for seventh through twelfth graders, and *Teacher Talk* for teachers or interested parents.

COMPUTER PALS AROUND THE WORLD

Computer Pals Around the World is a network which matches classrooms and schools from different states and countries using electronic mail as a medium. Once classrooms are matched, the classes then begin to exchange information, stories, class descriptions, or any material they desire through the use of a modem. Students are given the opportunity to write for a real audience. The program allows the individual teacher to integrate several different curriculum areas while providing the students with a meaningful learning activity.

How To

To get involved with this program, the teacher must first have the equipment necessary for electronic mail. A basic computer setup would involve a computer, a modem, phone lines, and the willingness to organize and motivate the students. Computer Pals Around the World offers a variety of tips and suggestions and is very willing to assist you in your individual needs. You will also need some funding and support from your local administration to cover the costs of using long distance phone lines.

Contact

> Computer Pals Around the World
> Alaska Sister Schools Network
> Office of Basic Education
> P.O. Box F
> Juneau, Alaska 99811
> (907) 465-2644

Variations

- *McGrath and Australia Students in Touch:* Students in McGrath use Computer Pals as a means of integrating curriculum in the area of geography. After making contact with a sister computer school in Australia, the students launched a project which involved five basic themes of geography. Students took photographs and wrote a booklet to share McGrath with their new friends in Australia. The students not only learned computer skills but also improved their writing skills and geography skills.

- *Bulletin Boards:* Students in Bud Kuenzli's classes have found the use of telecommunications in keeping touch with current events. The students call bulletin boards or electronic telecommunication services to access United Press International (UPI) or Associated Press International (API) news. The students use this information as a basis for studying current events in the classroom.

AUDIOCONFERENCING

Would you like your students to talk with teenagers in New York or Anchorage? Would you like them to hear from a university scientist about how sound from their boat travels through water? How about a conversation with Judy Blume or Kareem Abdul-Jabbar?

Audioconferencing is a cost-effective means of linking your students with resources far beyond the community and state. Many people all over the country would enjoy the opportunity to talk with culturally diverse students in Alaska. Call them! You'll be surprised to find out how willing they are to teach your students free of charge.

As *Learning through Audio Teleconferencing* (a Department of Education publication) points out, audioconferencing enables students:

1. To be active rather than passive learners.
2. To develop a sense of the people involved in abstract, distant events.
3. To use primary sources of information.

You can use audioconferencing in two ways: (1) You can expand your classroom by calling the person with whom you wish to speak and turning on your convenor, or (2) You can link your classroom with several locations in Alaska or outside the state by dialing into the bridge for connections. Several operators, located in Anchorage, operate the bridge. They connect the different sites into a conference and check the quality of the connections. They are available during the conference to help with technical problems.

Special conferencing equipment is available at more than 300 sites around the state. This portable equipment consists of a loudspeaker and a set of push-to-talk table microphones.

Many rural teachers participate in a statewide program using audioconferencing called the Battle of the Books (see description under Interdisciplinary Programs). Students read books from an assigned list and then participate in head-to-head competition with other schools via the audioconferencing system.

MIKE BELROSE

You can also arrange your own audioconferencing program. Students in the remote Aleutian village of Akutan, for example, held nine audioconferences with students and resource people all over Alaska. Audioconference topics included radio production, Native languages, and Alaska regional geography. Akutan students also produced a radio drama which they shared with a statewide student audience, again via audioconference.

How To

1. *Define the purpose and objectives.* Be specific about what you wish to achieve during the audioconference. Limit yourself to a few well-chosen and well thought-out objectives. Students should help in planning and goal-setting activities.

2. *Select and contact participants.* Contact participants at least three weeks in advance. Explain the purpose and objectives. Follow any telephone contacts with letters. Have your students write these letters.

3. *Prepare your students.* Work with students on preconference activities. These might include research, advance discussion, generating questions, and simulating the audioconference so they know what to expect.

4. *Prepare an agenda.* Involve students in preparing a written agenda that specifies the order of topics or questions, the process to be used, and the duration for each activity or objective.

5. *Limit the time.* Keep the conference to an hour or less. Keep in mind your students' attention span.

6. *Schedule the conference time.* At least one week in advance, contact the scheduler who will assign a bridge number.

7. *Inform participants.* Send the bridge number and the agenda to participants as much in advance as possible.

8. *Follow up.* Students could write letters to participants. Another follow-up activity could be putting together a magazine which contains responses of students and participants to the conference.

Variations

- *Hooking up with NASA:* Noatak High School students talked directly with a NASA research director at the Langley Research Center in Virginia about the space shuttle program. During the audioconference, students saw an accompanying slide show, took notes, and asked about space projects and career opportunities.

- *Audioconferencing on academics with other district students:* Students at Buckland High School participated in monthly audioconferences with students at other Northwest Arctic schools. Coordinated by the school district office, conferences focused on specific academic topics from science to literature.

- *University audioconference courses:* A student in Newhalen earned university credit by taking a history course via audioconference from the University of Alaska. The school's adult education coordinator supervised the student.

Contact

Office of Basic Education
Alaska Department of Education
Box F
Juneau, Alaska 99811
(907) 465-2884 or 465-2841

Write this office for a copy of their monograph, *Learning Through Audio Teleconferencing.* by Margorie M. Benning (1986). Alaska Department of Education, Office of Instructional Services.

INSTRUCTIONAL TELEVISION

Rural teachers have found instructional television of enormous value in opening up unfamiliar worlds to their students. Some teachers use television to teach entire courses to advanced students. Others use television to teach parts of courses, especially those requiring equipment and experimentation difficult in a small school.

Learning Through Television, a useful publication of the Office of Basic Education at Alaska's Department of Education, points out the special educational benefits possible through television. Television is particularly useful for transmitting concepts and information to students with limited reading skills. Alaska Native students tend to be strong visual learners, which makes televised lessons particularly attractive.

Television can bring to life abstract, remote material and personalize events distant in space and time. Students become engrossed in the action, color, and imagery.

At the same time, teachers know all too well that students have learned to be passive television viewers through constant exposure to entertainment television. To instruct effectively, teachers need to do much more than put in a videotape and let it run.

The Office of Instructional Delivery and Support (OIDS) has purchased the rights to over 160 ITV series—more than 3,000 individual programs in 13 curriculum areas. Most of them come with teacher's guides that suggest viewing activities, identify objectives, and describe the content of each program in the series. Some even have student workbooks, tests, maps, and computer software. Rural teachers have previewed ITV series by ordering the teacher's guide for review before ordering the tapes.

The most popular ITV programs among rural teachers are the Alaska studies programs: "Alaska History," "Alaska Native Land Claims Settlement Act Teacher In-Service," "Ecosystems of the Great Land," and "Sea School."

Other Alaska studies programs are also available. They include:

- *The Shadow Walkers*, a series about Alaska Native Cultures.

- *ANCSA: Caught in the Act*, a series designed for high-school students about the Alaska Native Claims Settlement Act.

- *Alaskan Sketches*, a series of biographical sketches of Alaskans who are successful in different careers and cultures.

Many teachers use programs from the Rural Alaska Television Network and the public broadcasters in their classes. Alaska's Public Broadcasting Stations also produce high quality programs on culture and current events. Examples of those programs are the award winning "Make Prayers to the Raven," a series about traditional beliefs of the Koyukuk people, and "We of the River," which documents the history of Natives in Southwest Alaska. Many of these programs are available through the state film library or through the producing station.

Rural teachers also make considerable use of programs in foreign languages, science, mathematical problem-solving, and reading.

Until 1986, ITV was delivered directly to rural schools through the LearnAlaska Instructional Television Network. Funding cuts have hampered direct delivery, although direct programming is now delivered via the Rural Alaska Television Network. Meanwhile, teachers can still obtain most of the ITV series from the State Film Library in Anchorage, if districts have contracted for services from the State Film Library.

How To

Interested in developing an effective television lesson? Here are some suggestions from *Learning Through Instructional Television*:

1. *Figure out just what you want the ITV materials to accomplish.* The programs can be used to introduce a unit, present the basic material, reinforce material, or set up a problem-solving situation. The teacher's guides contain valuable suggestions.

2. *Think creatively about how to group students.* You can set up an ITV center so that a student with headphones can use the programs independently. You can use the program for small student groups in a multi-level classroom. Sometimes the entire class will view the program, sometimes just a small group.

3. *Prepare students for what they will see on television.* Most students are not active viewers. Ask students to come up with questions about the content, or to make predictions about what they will see.

4. *Start and stop the tape to allow for reflection and discussion.* You do not need to play the program from start to finish. Stop the tape and talk about what has gone on. Ask students to anticipate what will be coming up. Review segments to check students' ideas or give them another chance to think through the question.

Contact

For a catalog and teacher's guides, write to or call:

Office of Basic Education
Alaska Department of Education
P.O. Box F
Juneau, Alaska 99811
(907) 465-2644

Ask OIDS as well for a copy of *Learning Through Instructional Television* by Marjorie Benning and the companion videotape, *Learning With Instructional Television.*

To borrow a tape, send a computerized request form to:

State Film Library
650 International Airport Road
Anchorage, Alaska 99502

Video in the School

The availability of videocassette recorders and cameras has created a great variety of learning opportunities for students in rural Alaska. In small schools, students have ready access to video equipment because of dramatically lower student-to-teacher and student-to-equipment ratios. The potential of this technology for use in the classroom is well illustrated by the work Bill Hatch did with his students at the St. George Island School.

Classroom Use. Hatch found that the opportunity to produce their own television programs was a powerful motivator for his students. When he encountered resistance from some shy students when they were assigned oral presentations, Bill worked out a compromise. Students made their presentations in front of the video camera. Then Bill and the students viewed the tape. "When they saw themselves, they viewed their performance critically," explained Hatch. "They then rewrote their speech and presented it again until they got it the way they wanted."

Video Productions. Hatch's students also produced their own ghostly video in an empty house. After editing and adding music, they submitted the tape to the Seward Silver Seahawk Video Festival. Against stiff competition that included much larger schools with more sophisticated equipment, they took second prize.

In addition to the ghost story, Hatch's students have produced other videos. They recorded a *bidar*, a wood-framed canvas boat large enough to hold a car, unloading supplies from a barge. The *bidar's* days ended with the completion of a new community dock. The tape represents an important historical record. The students sent the tape to a statewide television network news where it was edited and aired.

Video Yearbook. During the school year, students taped people, special events, wildlife, and village scenes. Then they edited their footage and added a soundtrack. "It's like a home movie for the whole village," explains Hatch.

Among the *educational benefits* of video production, Hatch includes:

BILL HATCH

- learning to plan, organize, speak, and write,
- learning to rewrite,
- building self-confidence and a sense of competence, and
- improving attitudes towards school and learning.

How To

Bill Hatch and Sylvia Gist, language arts teacher at St. Paul Island School, suggested the following in *Alaska Education News* (October 1985):

1. *Use high quality tapes and tape at your machine's highest speed.*

2. *Choose equipment carefully.* Purchase equipment that allows insert editing and recording of audio separately.

3. *Plan.* The more planning you do, the easier the project will be.

4. *Limit taping.* Hours of taping means hours of editing.

5. *Segment the project.* Produce your tape in short independent sections.

6. *Keep segments short.* Brevity keeps the video interesting.

7. *Trust students with equipment.*

8. *Assign tasks.* Make sure everyone on a video team has a role such as cameraperson or audio director.

9. *Think about sound.* Remote microphones make for better audio. Also, remind students to be conscious of the audio. One student ruined an hour of tape by humming during filming.

10. *Emphasize practice.* Give students plenty of opportunity to try out the equipment before beginning a project.

Variations

- *Public service commercials:* Marshall High School students produced a sixty-second animated public-service commercial on the dangers of drinking and driving. They constructed sets and a snowmachine from paper and used beer and liquor bottles as puppets. After taping, editing, and adding a music track, students sent the tape to KYUK in Bethel which aired it.

- *Video histories:* Marshall students also produced a video history of their village. After sketching out a script, they taped village elders and community scenes. As they edited the four hours of tape into a 45-minute show, they wove in old photographs, narration, music, and sound effects.

- *Exchange of videos with other schools:* Students at Central's Far North School produced a video of the Yukon Quest dog mushing race to exchange with high schools in Pennsylvania,

Nebraska, Oregon, other parts of Alaska, and elementary schools in Calgary, Canada.

- *Video yearbook production*: As a component of the Graphic Arts Class, high-school juniors and seniors in Atmautluak are writing copy, conducting interviews with village elders and school staff, learning video photography techniques, and editing a final copy that will be available in VHS format.

DISTANCE EDUCATION

Distance education has been around for a long time in the form of correspondence studies. Today schools are looking for higher technological delivery of courses to students. Distance education implies that the teacher and learners are separated by space and perhaps time, the instruction is carried by technological means, and two-way interaction exists to provide for clarification, feedback, and motivation.

Many teachers and administrators are looking at the delivery of classes by technology as a way to expand course offerings in small schools. Currently courses are being developed and offered via satellite transmission as well as other technologies in many lower 48 states.

Distance education can:

1. provide students with the opportunity to take courses not otherwise available to them,

2. allow students access to subject matter experts and individuals not available to them locally,

3. provide linkages to and opportunities for interaction with students in other schools,

4. make available to schools broad information and instructional resources such as data bases and computer networking,

5. increase educational quality in schools by providing opportunities for staff development and in-service training, and

6. develop increased community-based linkages.

Northwest Arctic School District has been experimenting with use of an electronic chalkboard in conjunction with Chukchi Campus for teaching a prealgebra course. The chalkboard system uses phone lines to transmit both audio and graphic information to students in the class. Students are also outfitted with the same equipment, so they can talk to as well as show the teacher their problems on the computer.

The Alaska Department of Education has developed a course in Alaska studies which uses computer activities, videotapes, print, and electronic mail. The *Alaska Studies Connection* is available to school districts either as a package to be taught by an on-site teacher or with complete teaching services provided by Centralized Correspondence Study.

The Alaska Department of Education is also participating in a five-year Star Schools project, funded by the federal government, which will significantly expand the impact of distance learning in the state. The Star Schools federal grant program provides demonstration grants for telecommunications partnerships to develop, construct, and acquire telecommunications facilities and equipment and to develop instructional programming to improve K–12 instruction in mathematics, science, and foreign languages.

The state departments of education in Alaska, Idaho, Montana, Oregon and Washington formed a partnership with the Satellite Telecommunications Educational Program (STEP) and Apple Computer, Inc. to apply for a Star Schools grant. The partnership was selected by the federal government to be awarded over $5 million for the first year; second-year funding is contingent upon reauthorization from the federal government.

The Pacific Northwest Star Schools partnership will develop and deliver these student courses to a total of 80 sites in Alaska (400 sites in the region) over the two years of the grant: summer basic skills, principles of technology, career paths, middle school science and technology, GED, and applied mathematics. The sites chosen to participate were selected on the basis of need, however, priority was given to rural and remote sites.

The project will also provide in-service training through satellite to site staff and support from the Alaska Department of Education for technical assistance to the sites, as well as information dissemination about telecommunications.

The system that the grant is funding will allow for data and graphics transmission over the satellite band width to students in the classes as well as transmission of individual assignments or grades. The computer link will allow for the return of information and homework assignments from the students back to the teachers electronically within 24 hours.

Contact

District approval and support is essential for any distance delivery course. For more information on distance education, contact:
Office of Basic Education
Alaska Department of Education
P. O. Box F
Juneau, Alaska 99811
(907) 465-2644

■ Take a Fresh Look at Scheduling

BLOCK SCHEDULING

The conventional seven-period school day often does not fit the needs of curriculum and instruction in small schools. Many rural teachers are tailoring time to the curriculum. By innovative scheduling, teachers can also use community people as teachers and reduce the number of their daily class preparations.

In Dot Lake, the principal/teacher adopted block scheduling for certain kinds of intensive courses. Each course met, for example, two and a half hours per day for 12 weeks or 150 hours total over 12 weeks rather than the conventional 36 weeks. Dot Lake offered students nine courses in a school year. A typical cluster was biology, Spanish I, and American government. There are further advantages of block scheduling of intensive courses:

- *More courses may be offered.* Community members who could not commit nine months to teaching may be able to teach for three. An additional benefit is the strengthening of school-community relations by using community members as instructors.

- *Course rotation helps maintain student interest and fosters high attendance.* Kids are less restive at the end of the year because they're not banging their heads against the same old thing. They do, of course, tire of intensive courses as well, but by the time they begin to complain, it's all over.

- *If students drop out of school during the year, all is not lost.* They will receive credit for the intensive courses they have completed successfully.

- *Instruction time is increased* due to a reduction of total class time being used on set up and wrap up.

Variations

- *Minicourses:* At Togiak Junior High School, during first period, students are divided among physical education, art, music, and vocational education. Students attend each course for three weeks and then rotate to the next course. At the end of twelve weeks, each student will have had a mini-course in each of the four subjects.

- *Block Minicourses:* For one week each spring in Akutan, students enjoy a "minisession and educational fair." After attending required classes in reading, math, and cultural arts in the morning, students spend the afternoon in elective courses such as drafting, fencing, and puppetry. These electives are scheduled in blocks of from 15 minutes to three hours, depending on the subject. On the weekend, students present their completed projects to the community.

  Students in the minicourse on geography, for example, presented a map and a written profile of Akutan. Students in the minicourse in journalism presented a mock news program. The program breaks the routine and rekindles student interest.

Explore the Education Available
in the Community

This chapter looks at different ways of using the community to educational advantage:

- Using local talent
- Developing cultural heritage projects
- Providing community services
- Starting student enterprises

The most important resource for rural teachers (outside of themselves) is the local community. Teachers can employ community members as classroom resource people who possess a range of skills and knowledge about subsistence, survival, craft skills, local ecosystems, local history, and traditional stories and dance. Local instructors offer another enormous advantage: they embody and express community values.

Many rural teachers are developing curriculum and projects that tie into the traditions, customs, economy, and history of the local community. Such activities build upon students' familiarity with local subjects and their interest in their immediate world. By demonstrating to the community that the school considers the community a vital element in educating youth, these activities also generate local support for the school and the academic program.

Teachers can also build upon and develop a central value of rural Alaska: serving the community first. Projects that provide services to the community both strengthen this value and, again, develop support for the school in the community.

EMPLOYING COMMUNITY PEOPLE TO WORK IN THE SCHOOL

Three of the most common criticisms of small schools are (1) the lack of variety in the curriculum, (2) the lack of variety in teachers, and (3) teachers teaching subjects for which they are not qualified. By using local instructors, the school can address all three problems.

When a 1984 community survey revealed that parents in Dot Lake wanted their children to study a foreign language, for example, the principal hired a local resident who was a native speaker of Spanish with some teaching experience at the college level. The Spanish class was so successful that all eight students signed up for Spanish II.

Kwigillingok High School hired the village corporation president to teach an Alaska Native Land Claims and corporation management course. To teach aerospace science, Birch Creek School hired a local pilot.

When the students at Port Alsworth wanted to learn how to build dogsleds, the school hired Nels Hedlund. During the last period each day, Nels demonstrated construction to the junior high students. For two hours each day, both during and after school, the students worked on their own sled. In ten days, they completed a sled that they raffled off for $1,200.

Dan Hill, former principal at Port Alsworth, feels the real payoff came when one of the students helped his father make a sled. The boy was able to show his father that he had learned something useful in school.

How To

1. *Involve your constituents.* What do your students want to learn about? What do parents want their children to learn? Dan suggests that you "keep your ear to the ground. You'll hear kids say that they wish they could learn about airplanes or guns or whatever." Parents, too, will voice their wishes for their children, often informally over tea or during bingo. So be prepared to listen.

2. *Identify the right person.* After identifying areas of interest, talk with local residents working at the school, school committee members, the mayor, and village council president. They will know who in the community could teach the subject.

3. *Determine a reasonable compensation.* Figure out how much you can pay people before you approach them. Veteran teachers point out that you risk insulting people if you are not prepared to pay them. As teachers are paid for teaching their expertise, local people justifiably expect to be paid for teaching their expertise. To avoid putting people on the spot, particularly if you are new to the community, you might wish to mention the possibility of teaching casually and in a indirect manner. The individual's response to the suggestion will cue you as to whether or not you should pursue the idea further.

   Because he had spent several years in the community and had hired several local people to teach, Dan Hill was able to approach potential teachers directly: "I happened to notice you have a lot of skill in (whatever). Have you ever considered that a lot of students could benefit from your skill?"

4. *Organize clearly.* A written description of the course with stated objectives is important. Such a document constitutes a kind of contract with the teacher and can be shown to district officials to justify the expense. Some local teachers will be comfortable writing up their own course descriptions. With others, you may wish to have them describe the course and the objectives and you write these down. Read them back to the teacher to ensure that you have understood each other.

5. *Determine student credit.* Figure out the number of hours needed for students to earn 1/4 credit or 1/2 credit. If the teachers cannot devote the 34 or 67 hours necessary for credit, you may have to classify the course as extracurricular.

6. *Train the teachers.* This is a delicate matter. Remember that you have hired these individuals as experts. To take the attitude that you are going to show them how to teach is to risk insulting them. Traditional methods of teaching, which are indirect and involve observation and independent practice, may conflict with your expectations. In Newtok, Jim Strohmer worked with his aide, John Charles, to develop an elective course on subsistence skills and lifestyle. Before class, Jim and John would sit down and design the lesson together. Then John would teach the lesson. This type of cooperation and sharing of information and experience worked well.

7. *Help out with instruction.* Make sure that the materials the local teacher needs are available and ready. Be available in case the local teacher needs assistance. If possible, attend his classes.

8. *Show your appreciation.* Discuss with your students an appropriate token of appreciation. This may be a gift the students have made or selected, a party, or a certificate.

Variations

• *Training for local teachers:* Yukon Flats School District established a Village Teachers Training Program at the district's Vocational Education Center in 1984. Skilled adults who want to teach in the vocational education program at their local high school were able to apply for admission to the program. Those chosen by the local school committee or those promised a job by the high school or village corporation then received more training in their speciality and attended classes on teaching methods, curriculum, and lesson design.

The center also provided career guidance. Participants developed a lifetime placement file. This file contained a standardized registration form, an academic aptitude profile, an inventory of career interests, a record of their

NORTH SLOPE BOROUGH SCHOOL DISTRICT

training at the center, and a list of skills they had demonstrated.

When they had completed the program at the center, the teachers returned to teach in their villages. Thanks to the program, for the first time, some students in Yukon Flats were able to receive vocational training in their schools. Unfortunately, this program is no longer available, but it does provide a model for other school districts.

- *Home-school coordinator:* At the Joann Alexie Memorial School in Atmautlauk, village elder Oscar Nick is assigned as the home-school coordinator for one period daily. In this role, he assists the school counselor in working with students and encouraging dropouts to return to school, and he visits the homes of truant and tardy students.

■ Students Learn About Their Cultural Heritage

A false dichotomy has been created between programs designed to teach conventional academic skills and knowledge on the one hand, and programs designed to teach Native students about the history, customs, crafts, and values of their people on the other.

These objectives are equally important and mutually supportive. Yet some people see them as incompatible.

The evidence shows these programs are complementary. The work of John Pingayak and Joseph Slats in Chevak, as an example, demonstrates that excellence in one type of program does not preclude excellence in the other.

THE CHEVAK CULTURAL HERITAGE PROGRAM

"If we want our young to be strong, they must have a sense of their past. The school is obligated to fill the hole it created in the learning of traditional skills and values." This is the way John Pingayak described the motivation behind the Cultural Heritage Program.

The program today has its own building in part of the old BIA school and two elders who serve as consultants and provide information on local history and genealogy. "The elders are our connection between what happened in the old days and modern times. They are the only ones who know what happened," explained John.

The elders also play a key role as conflict mediators. They talk to whole classes about the importance of education and maintenance of the knowledge and skills of their people. They are a vital link between the school and the community, the past and the present, the young and the old. Before the program began, John's grandfather, Joe Friday, fulfilled this role.

John taught cultural heritage in grades three through six as well as in two high-school classes. The program offered instruction in traditional skills such as carving, skin sewing,

FAIRBANKS DAILY NEWS-MINER

Eskimo dance, and subsistence as well as in local history. Students have produced videotapes, Native-language textbooks for elementary students, and dance theater. John arranged a trip to Russia for his dance group.

Each spring, the program organized the annual Spring Dance Awareness Festival. In the mornings, students attended their regular classes but worked on topics with cultural themes. Visiting students from other schools often joined them. A morning spent studying nonverbal communication skills might be followed by an afternoon of traditional stories or a discussion of local history in the village church.

In the evening the students, together with visitors and community members, gathered in the community hall for Eskimo dancing to the drumming and chanting of the elders.

How To

John offers the following advice for those interested in cultural heritage programs. He credits his grandfather, Joe Friday, with these ideas.

1. *Show respect to the elders.* "In every village, show respect to the elders if you are looking for information from them."

2. *Treat the elders as professionals.* "Hire the elders to work in the school not as aides but as professionals. You are asking for help; you should respect their knowledge."

3. *Open the school to the village.* "You must believe that the school is an intricate part of the village. Some schools have a closed-door policy. But the best policy is open door. The school should be a community building." While John doesn't have the financial resources to travel widely, he is willing to come and answer questions if transportation is provided. Those who would like to see how the Chevak program works are encouraged to come visit during the spring festival.

The St. Lawrence Island Yup'ik Language and Culture Curriculum

The program was initiated in 1984 to develop a course of studies that would integrate Yup'ik culture into the educational program in a way that would encourage relevant learning, particularly in the area of language skills. The program is implemented at the district level in grades K–12 with the high-school portion consisting of a curriculum guide and three textbooks. The texts are written in Yup'ik and English and a library of 35 video tapes is available that covers a wide range of culturally related topics and activities for use in the classroom.

Contact

Director, Special & Transitional Programs
Bering Strait School District
P.O. Box 225
Unalakleet, Alaska 99684
(907) 624-3611

Variations

- *Cultural heritage minicourses:* For three weeks, Togiak students worked with elders to plan and carry out projects on subsistence, local archaeological sites, ivory carving, kayak building, and Eskimo Olympics and dancing. At the culminating culture fair, students present their projects to the community.

- *Native arts week:* Mekoryuk, Kasigluk, Goodnews Bay, Nulato, and other villages hold Native Arts Weeks similar to Togiak. Sometimes regular classes are interrupted for a week. In some schools, elders take over and teach classes.

- *Native language and cultural skills combo:* In Shishmaref, a community expert taught ivory carving. The students learn their language as they learn to carve by speaking only Inupiaq.

- *Community photograph gallery:* Emmonak High School students collected old photographs from friends and relatives. Students made frames for prints of the photos. Prints were then displayed at the school.

CURT MADISON

- *Community museum:* Using artifacts donated by community members and teachers or purchased by the school, students at Alak High School in Wainwright have created a museum in the school's commons area.

- *Local student-published books:* Students at Akula High School in Kasigluk published three books on local traditions. To gather information, students interviewed elders and other experts. They also took and developed photographs for the books. Modeled on the *Foxfire* series, each book focused on a single theme: Tundra Fishing in Akula, Skin Sewing and Clothing in Akula, and Past Times and Recreations in Akula. The Lower Kuskokwim School District print shop did final editing, layout, and printing.

- *Trapping skills in vocational education:* In Chignik Lake, students took a vocational education course that covered not only the techniques of trapping, tanning, and sewing hides but animal habitat and behavior as well. Students and their teacher set up a trapline about ten miles from the school. Under the supervision of local school aides, students regularly checked the traps.

- *Outdoor skills and hunting and trapping program:* Students in Atmautluak's Outdoor Skills and Hunting and Trapping Program went on five-day moose hunts. During the hunt they slept in earth shelters; stalked, shot, and butchered a moose; and did some fishing. As preparation for the hunt, students learned about gun safety, hunting, and trapping in their vocational education class.

- *Trapping field trips:* Circle High School students spent three days at a local trapper's cabin. They learned to set up a tent, build a fire, find water, snare muskrat and beaver, skin animals, and tan hides.

- *Listening, telling, and preserving program:* The Lake and Peninsula School District has set up a program where junior and senior high-school students interview local people and produce a book of interviews called *Now, Then, and Forever.*

- *Elders we admire:* One class at the Russian Mission School in the Lower Yukon School District chooses an elder in the village that they admire, interviews the elder, and writes a report based on the tape recording.

- *Cultural arts week:* As a part of the Cultural Arts Week, village elders in Atmautluak are hired for a week of instruction in traditional skills including kayak construction, net mending, trap making, *uluaq* making, skin sewing, basket weaving, knitting, *kuspuk* sewing, string stories, and Eskimo dancing.

- *Native language day:* Students and community members participate in a Native Language Day in Anaktuvuk Pass. The language teachers initiate this program in connection with a cultural day to teach the students about the local culture. Local people also participate by teaching classes in skinning, the Inupiaq writing system, bread making, Eskimo dancing, and the messenger feast.

■ Students Serve the Community

The relationship between the school and the community should not be one way. Just as the community can provide a rich resource for the school, so the school can provide vital services to the community.

In providing services such as small engine repair, snack bars, and community newspapers, students learn important skills as well as the value of community service. Such services bring the community and school closer together.

A Repair and Construction Facility for the School and Community

---

King Cove students opened a repair shop for the community. The school needed additional shop equipment and shop space. The community needed a site and tools to repair equipment, appliances, and furniture. The school board provided funds to purchase construction materials—and the high-school shop class and maintenance personnel did the rest. Together they built the entire facility except for pouring the concrete floor and wiring the addition.

The school was then able to offer two additional shop classes. One was in small-engine repair. The other was an open-shop class during which students could work on a project of their own choosing. Students worked on three-wheel ATVs, constructed and repaired equipment for fishing boats, repaired trucks and cars, and built or repaired furniture.

During nonschool hours, the school makes the shop available to the community. The shop instructor supervises the shop after hours. The school reports few problems with lost or damaged equipment.

How To

1. *Find the right shop teacher.* The critical ingredient is a shop teacher who knows the community well and knows the type of work the community needs.

2. *Build on the industrial arts/vocational education program.* Repair and construction activities are a natural extension of the school program. In most rural communities the school will not be competing with local businesses.

3. *Plan for problems.* Tools, equipment, and materials have legs of their own. Think of an appropriate means of accounting for such items. Shop supervision is the school's responsibility. Your program must take this into account.

Variations

- *Building projects with local materials:* In Chalkyitsik, students built a log house and a large frame shed. Before beginning the projects, they built a scale model. Students selected, felled, and peeled logs for the log house. They built the shed according to national building codes, using fire stops, insulation, and flame-proof materials for roofing.

  The use of power equipment, cautioned Principal Peter Van Borkulo, required close supervision of students. Village adults provided additional instruction and supervision. The building projects even attracted dropouts who were paired with current students serving as peer tutors.

- *Greenhouses in winter:* Students in Ft. Yukon built a greenhouse that would later be used to teach a horticulture class. The students drew the plans and then built a scale model. Because the greenhouse was being built at the Vocational Education Center, the students also had to build a skid to move the finished greenhouse to the school. Students were responsible for framing, insulating, and wiring the building and expect to grow plants, flowers, and vegetables year round.

- *Finishing construction on the school:* Pitkas Point needed a new elementary school. The district had funds to build a single-story, 2,700-square-foot building. Instead, they chose to build a two-story building with a 2,400-square-foot bottom floor and an unfinished top floor.

  The school hired a high-school teacher who had home-building skills. The next year he and the vocational education students finished the top floor. The students and teacher ordered all the materials, drew up plans for the fire marshall, helped the electrician do the wiring, hung the doors, installed the windows, put up the Sheetrock, taped and textured the walls, did the painting, made and installed the trim, and laid the carpet.

The school gained 4,400 square feet of floor space. The students gained a variety of useful building skills.

COMMUNITY PROFILES

Nelson Lagoon had no official post office. Mail went to Cold Bay and was brought to the village twice weekly by air. The mail went to the community building, was sorted by an unpaid community member, and then was placed in open cubicles. Neither the building nor the cubicles were secure. Mail was often slow and sometimes was routed to other communities that share Nelson Lagoon's zip code.

When the head teacher learned that the community could submit a proposal to the district postmaster for a contract post office, he asked students to do the groundwork for such a proposal.

Typically, proposals for government contracts require a community profile. Students took as their model an outdated profile compiled by the Arctic Environmental Information and Data Center (AEIDC). Using more current studies and local sources, students gathered information on local government, the economy, the environment, the population, and educational facilities. Students entered their data on microcomputers using word-processing programs. They drew a map of the community and photographed community structures. Ultimately the Nelson Lagoon Post Office was opened.

The Aleutian Regional School Board was so impressed with the student's work that they adopted the profiles as an Indian Education project. Now all six schools in the district have developed profiles.

How To

1. *Look at your curriculum.* To fit the project into the existing curriculum, look at your curriculum objectives and determine just what you want your project to accomplish.

2. *Coordinate planning with other teachers.* To work, the project requires the cooperation of other faculty. If you can sell them the idea, they will be able to suggest ways of working project activities into their classes.

3. *Discuss the project with your students.* Again, you may need to sell them on the idea. Once they've bought it, they will suggest ways of gathering and presenting information.

4. *Use the project as an opportunity for writing.* The Nelson Lagoon project used ideas from the Alaska Writing Project. Students wrote sections of the profile in editorial teams.

5. *Locate different sources of information.* The University of Alaska has a wealth of information on rural Alaska, including aerial photographs and environmental impact studies. Village and regional corporations are also good sources. The profiles compiled by AEIDC, mentioned above, are yet another source. Contact the Alaska Department of Community and Regional Affairs in Juneau.

6. *Take breaks.* Students should not work continuously on the project. Rather, work on the project for a week and do something else for a couple of weeks before returning to the project.

7. *Enter the information on a computer.* This enables students to update the profile easily and quickly. Using a graphics program, students would also be able to add charts and graphs to the profile.

The School/Community Newspaper

While school newspapers are fairly common, in small rural communities they serve an unusual function: the school newspaper is often the only community newspaper.

For example, the Shishmaref School's newsletter keeps residents informed about upcoming events as well as school news. The principal writes a regular column on concerns such as attendance.

Many school papers go well beyond school matters, offering articles on community meetings and events, on health, and on local economic activities. The papers also carry advertising for local businesses.

A school newspaper that publishes articles of interest to the community strengthens ties between the school and community. Such a paper signals residents that the school recognizes the importance of community events and concerns.

How To

1. *Don't worry about your limited expertise.* If students start up the paper and decide on content and format, they will be more enthusiastic. Your lack of experience is an opportunity for them.

2. *This is a low-budget activity.* With the computer software now available and copying machines in all schools, you can publish a paper very inexpensively.

3. *Start simply.* Your primary objective should be just to get the paper out so everyone knows it exists.

4. *Identify and appeal to your readership's interests.* Roberta Ward in Kaltag warns that what interests the teacher may not strike students and community members as newsworthy. Coverage of local sports events is a sure winner. "Check out ideas for stories with aides and elders," advises Ward. Finally, allow students to decide what to publish.

5. *Be flexible.* The typical format of regular columns may not meet your readership's expectations—as Bonnie and Dave Evans discovered in Koyukuk. Working with their aides, Shirley Huntington and Josie, Marie, and Agnes Dayton, they changed the format of the weekly *Raider Review.* Each issue now focuses on one theme or subject such as whales.

6. *Incorporate the writing process.* The Evanses follow the process taught through the Alaska Writing Consortium. On Monday, students brainstorm articles and do quickwriting.

On Tuesday, students (in pairs) give feedback on one another's work and revise. On Wednesday, students (in teams of three or four) check the grammatical correctness of articles. On Thursday, students do final revisions on Macintosh computers. Friday is layout, print, and distribution day.

Public Speaking for a Purpose

Leona Grishkowsky, a teacher at Unalakleet High School, has come up with an innovative way to involve students in public speaking. By using the local basketball season as the stage, Leona has involved her students in all aspects of public speaking.

During the basketball season, students interact with players, coaches, and staff to obtain information they need to prepare the pregame show announcements and introductions during the games. In addition, the students are exposed to typewriters, computers, public announcement systems, and public broadcasting during the games. Students are not only learning valuable skills in public speaking but they are also having fun.

The program has been continued and expanded to include activities all through the year. Students announce wrestling tournaments, gymnastics exhibitions, etc. Some of the students in speech classes must perform at least once in order to meet class requirements directed by the curriculum.

Contact

Bering Strait School District Office
P.O. Box 225
Unalakleet, Alaska 99684
(907) 624-3611, extension 231

■ Student Entrepreneurship Programs

Teachers and students in small schools have started a number of different businesses in their communities such as restaurants, bakeries, stores, and snack bars. These enterprises provide students with practice in a variety of skills and also provide useful goods and services for the community. Other small schools have developed programs that directly teach students skills important in the local economy and business world.

The Wainwright High School Corporation

In Wainwright, students become shareholders in their own profit-making corporation. They own and operate wholesale businesses for Native crafts, tapes and albums, and soda drinks. They have also organized a regular movie night, dances, raffles, and invitational basketball tournaments.

Profits are used to pay students for after-school and weekend work. Profits are also used to begin new business activities and make new investments. Last summer, three students on the board of directors journeyed to Anchorage to negotiate purchase of a rental unit.

The Wainwright High School Student Corporation is one of eight student corporations in the North Slope School District. The corporations are patterned after the regional and village corporations established by the Alaska Native Claims Settlement Act.

How To

1. *Issue stock.* Each student is issued 100 shares—valued at $1 per share—by the local school board. Stocks can be traded, sold, or bought among shareholders.

2. *Set up a corporate organization.* During a shareholders' meeting, shareholders elect a board of directors. A faculty advisor works with the board to manage the corporation.

The board sets goals and policies. The board also selects a president and other corporate officials.

3. *Write a handbook.* The district publishes a Student Corporation Handbook that includes the articles of incorporation and bylaws and that orients students and teachers to the student corporations.

4. *Seek legal counsel before beginning.* Student shareholders are minors under state law and need adult agents to assume responsibility for their actions as shareholders. The corporations are incorporated under state law, have their own business licenses, are governed by state corporate law, and must file federal income tax returns.

Contact

Johnnie Lee
Program Coordinator
North Slope Borough School District
Barrow, Alaska 99
(907) 852-5311

INTERNATIONAL TRADE

Working in cooperation with vocational programs and Native arts instruction, Dora Cline (Dillingham City School District) developed a Pacific Rim Entrepreneurship Program that provided students with entrepreneurship education and attempted to establish an export enterprise with a sister school in China. Their objectives were (1) to secure overseas trading, (2) to engage students in entrepreneurship competencies through actual business activities and (3) to use traditional skills such as skin sewing for trading purposes.

Small Businesses

- *Native and graphic arts:* Another district in southeast Alaska (Wrangell High School) provided small business curriculum in conjunction with Native and graphic arts. Art teacher Kirk Garbisch engaged 22 students in designing silk screen prints and copper embossings for the tourism trade. They worked with retail outlets both within their own community and in other southeast communities to market their projects. Curriculum content centered on (1) acquiring identified entrepreneurship skills (*18 Modules—Pace Materials: Program for Acquiring Competencies in Entrepreneurship*, Ohio State University, 614-292-4353 and *Risks and Rewards*), (2) acquiring and enhancing artistic skills, and (3) using Native and graphic arts.

- *Industrial ice picks:* The Kuspuk School District through their vocational technical center at Aniak and the leadership of Roger Prator, industrial arts teacher, integrated entrepreneurship skills in their industrial arts program, producing and selling industrial-quality ice picks to vendors in Anchorage. Teachers were intent upon students not only acquiring specific technical and artistic skills, but also learning specific business and communication skills.

- *Small manufacturing:* Bering Strait industrial education and home economics teachers Steve Noonkesser and Lori Brewer at Teller introduced basic concepts of business operation to their students by organizing and operating a small manufacturing business. Students produced small wooden toys, ceramic items, tailored goods, and home decorating products. The small business allowed students to supplement existing vocational courses by applying skills learned in classes, to explore alternative means of earning an income, and to acquire basic business start-up skills.

- *Community analysis:* Both Todd Bergman of New Stuyahok and Ron Gibbs of Ouzinkie and Port Lyons have developed model programs for their students to understand how to establish small business enterprises. Their students had the opportunity to conduct thorough community market analyses that could result in viable business plans for potential school-based enterprises. The students were able to apply skills acquired in their small business management classes to an actual business start-up project.

JOAN WALSER

- *A story-knife business:* In Kipnuk, students sell story-knives. Each packet contains a hand-carved story-knife, examples of stories told using the knife, and illustrations. The school can't keep up with demand.

- *A restaurant business:* Students in Selawik ran a restaurant after school as part of their Work Experience Program. Freshmen learn how the restaurant operates and explore career options. Sophomores serve as cooks and maintain the restaurant. Juniors are the cashiers, work at the counter, and study advertising, retail operations, math, and human relations. Seniors, as befits their exalted station in life, manage the operation. Before the Selawik program began, less than 20 percent of the high-school graduates went on to take a job or to attend postsecondary training. Now more than half do so.

- *A bakery business:* Russian Mission students started a community bakery. They baked cookies, bread, and cakes and took special orders for special occasions.

- *New Stuyahok enterprises:* Students in New Stuyahok are in the process of researching, planning, and starting a licensed, student-owned small business. Teacher

Todd Bergman is assisting his students in all aspects of starting a business, including establishing community interest, securing in-kind funding, and finding potential locations.

Other Business Ideas

Day care center	Crafts guild
Elders service	Greenhouse products
Garbage collection	Sled kits
Snowmachine repair	Diaper service
Fix-it shop	Gun-cleaning service
Local cookbook	Firewood service
Fur factory	Bakery
Pet and plant service	Tape and CD sales
Tax service	Recycling service
Travel agency	Foraging products
Boat supply	Tourist services
Jams and jellies	Snack shop
Tutoring service	Call and haul
Computer services	Film and photo service
Video rental	T-shirts and button sales

Contact

Office of Adult Vocational Education
Alaska Department of Education
P.O. Box F
Juneau, Alaska 99811
(907) 465-4685

Other Resources

The *Program for Acquiring Competence in Entrepreneurship (PACE)* can help you establish an individualized entrepreneurship curriculum designed to meet your needs.

Program Information Office
National Center for Research in Vocational Education
1960 Kenny Road
Columbus, OH 43210
(800) 848-4815

Commercial Fisheries Apprenticeship Program

The Commercial Fisheries Apprenticeship Program in Cordova, Alaska, is designed to prepare students to enter the fishing industry and get a limited entry permit. It is designed as a three-year program, though some students may want to take longer. Students take a variety of courses at the high school and college during the school year and work on fishing vessels during the summer.

Strong community support together with the enthusiasm of students, teachers, administration, and school board makes the program work. It began with a meeting of city, school district, college, marine advisory, and fishing organization representatives. The program used seed money from the city, the fishing organization, the community college, and a grant from the Office of Adult and Vocational Education to get started. A coordinator was hired to head the program. Another key to the program is the community advisory board, a subcommittee of the school board which meets monthly through the school year.

The fisheries program is interdisciplinary, with fisheries topics integrated into a number of classes at the junior and senior high schools. Each semester one class is offered specifically for fisheries students. Other offerings include evening classes at the college and short courses for the community on topics such as marine electrical systems, marine hydraulics, welding, marine engines, and financial management.

For the students, the hands-on part of the program is their favorite—going on field trips, working on fishing boats, welding a river skiff, taking apart an engine, learning knots and splices, mending and hanging nets, using electronics, and talking to the experts from the fishing industry who instruct or assist with instruction in their classes. Insurance for field trips and the fishing experience has been one difficulty for many school districts. James, Inc. of Seattle helped obtain an extra $700,000 of liability so that the program could have $1 million worth of coverage for each student on field trips and for the summer's fishing experience. The University of Alaska has field trip insurance that helps with coverage on classes taught through the university system. Insurance is also easier to obtain if the school owns its own boat. This year, both a 28-foot bowpicker and a 16-foot jitney were donated to the program. Two school districts are building their own boats, and one other district had a boat purchased by their borough.

For the first two years, the program was funded primarily by grants from the Office of Adult and Vocational Education. Presently, primary funding comes from an Educational Limited Entry Permit. These permits are available from the Limited Entry Commission on a yearly basis to schools with valid fisheries education programs. The program chartered captains and boats for seine and gillnet operations, paid the students stipends, and funded the wintertime fisheries program: classes, books, videos, net mending supplies, safety equipment, and field trips. The money cannot be used for the purchase of boats or for major capital expenditures, and any remaining money is returned to the state.

In Cordova, the vocational fisheries program gives students a chance to become fishers in a safe and professional manner. The fishing industry is the largest employer in the state. The program works to increase the self-confidence, seamanship skills, fisheries techniques, and knowledge of fisheries management—so that these young people will be better able to manage our Alaskan natural resources.

Contact

Belle Mickelson
Cordova City Schools
Box 140
Cordova, Alaska 99574-0140
(907) 424-3265

3

Broaden Students' Experience
with Travel Programs

Moving Right Along

In this chapter, we explore how rural teachers use the opportunity to travel with their students to

- broaden the students' experience of the world,
- teach the students unfamiliar concepts,
- help the students acquire a more realistic picture of contemporary American life, and
- give the students an opportunity to make better judgements on what they want to do after high school.

The isolation of rural villages leads small school teachers to seek ways of broadening their students' experience of the world. Many teachers see the opportunity to travel with their students as one of the great advantages of small schools. With 17 students, not 1,700, everything is manageable.

Some rural school districts have travel policies built around a "travel scope and sequence." Younger students go to Anchorage or Fairbanks to get first-hand experience in a city. Older students travel outside Alaska so they can better understand contemporary American life. High-school seniors go on a tour of colleges and vocational schools so they can make better judgments about what to do after high school.

In other districts, teachers are on their own. Some teachers plan an entire academic year around a big study trip.

■ **Organizing Study Trips**

FT. YUKON STUDENTS SEE AMERICA ON A GREYHOUND BUS

Bill Pfisterer and Carolyn Peter, former teachers at the Ft. Yukon School, met with the parents of their 36 Athabaskan students and jointly planned a cross-country tour. They structured the tour around Greyhound's special 35-day "Ameripass." Pfisterer, Peter, and a half dozen parents accompanied the students. To save money, they traveled at night and slept on the bus.

They toured a furniture factory on an Indian reservation in the Southwest, saw a calf born on a Midwestern dairy farm, and didn't forget to stop at Disneyland. In Ohio, the students visited pen pals who had earlier trekked north to Alaska. They stayed in their pen pals' homes and swam in swimming pools.

On the East Coast, they hiked along trails in the Great Smokey Mountains and toured historical sites in Washington, D.C. When they returned to Ft. Yukon, they had more experience of the United States and its diversity than most of their counterparts in large urban schools.

The trip that Bill, Carolyn, and the Ft. Yukon parents organized illustrates the benefits of such student travel. Students experience first hand many of the places, events, and concepts that they read about in textbooks. Such travel also helps dispel students' sense of isolation. They are able to see the similarities, as well as the differences, between their way of life and that of others. They get a much more realistic picture of the world than the one that comes across on the television screen.

Finally, travel helps students to put their own experience into perspective. They are better able to see the options and alternatives open to them. Whether they choose to stay in Ft. Yukon to fish and trap or whether they choose to leave to take a salaried job, they will have had a chance to see what is over the mountain.

How To

For the following suggestions, we are indebted to Bill Pfisterer, Glenys Bowerman, and the students of Ft. Yukon.

1. *Get ready.* At least three options are available for organizing the trip. First, you can work through a travel agent. Second, you can sign up for a prepackaged tour. Such tours are available to just about anywhere in the world. Third, you can plan the trip yourself, which is what Bill Pfisterer and Carolyn Peter did. "Get the students involved," says Bill. Have them write to the chambers of commerce in the cities you are thinking of visiting. Have them contact a local school in the city. Send the school a video of your school, the students, and the village. Have them work out a schedule, computing travel time and mileage to different cities as well as the money needed. As they are learning to arrange travel, they are also reading, writing, and calculating. Not bad for what some critics call a "frill."

2. *Getting together the wherewithal.* With Indian Education and Johnson-O'Malley funds, as well as oil revenues, fast drying up, self-reliance is yet another lesson students can learn from travel. Noatak students held a carnival and raised $4,000 in two nights. Nenana students have managed to raise $3,400 each during the last two years. Ft. Yukon students supplemented funds provided by the BIA to amass nearly $30,000 for their cross-country jaunt. Here are some ideas:

   • *Food*
   Yes, the ubiquitous bake-sale is tried and true—but think on a grander scale: open a student store during recreation hours. Serve cinnamon rolls and juice in a morning

"wake-up-teria." Run concessions for sporting events and cook meals for visiting teams.

- *Information*
Put together a cookbook of local recipes and sell it. Students in Nenana collected recipes—including a sure winner, "Polar Bear Grunt Stew"—and had a local artist draw a picture for the cover. The book was printed inexpensively by a printer in Tennessee.

- *Stage special events*
Noatak students built booths for their Senior Carnival and ordered raffle prizes. The whole community turned out to play games, eat, and swell the travel kitty. For more ideas, contact Glenys Bowerman at Nenana High School who has generously offered her help.

3. *Getting ready academically.* This is an opportunity for true interdisciplinary studies. In social studies, students can learn about the geography, culture, and economy of the places they are to visit. In math, they can compute expenses, mileage, and per student cost. In science, they can learn about the technology of industries and mining in the places they are to visit. In art and music, they can study regional art works, architecture, artists and composers. In English, they can write letters to inquire about the places they will visit. The possibilities are almost limitless.

4. *Setting off.* Have plenty of chaperones. Think carefully about an appropriate "span of supervision." Ft. Yukon had eight adults for 36 students. Frank Mitchell took five adults to supervise 26 students from the Iditarod School District. In other words, plan for one adult for each group of five or six students. Students should learn about how to act with strangers, how to act in public places, and how to address people in various positions. Students who are unfamiliar with traffic should learn some rules for pedestrians. Prepare students for accidental separation. Tell them how to find the police or, if in a foreign country, the American embassy. Each student should also have an itinerary that includes the address and phone number of their lodgings each night for the entire trip. (For additional information see Urban Survival Skills in chapter 7.)

YUKON KOYUKUK SCHOOLS

5. *During the trip.* Organize a system for accounting for students. You may want to have students wear bright sweatshirts or jackets so they can be easily spotted and can spot one another. Before arriving at each destination, review with the students the behavior expected of them. Point out local cultural rules. Chaperones may also need this information. An outraged ranger in the Smoky Mountains apprehended a parent-chaperone who had cut down a tree to make a clothesline. Have students take along some small, inexpensive gifts that they can give as tokens of appreciation. Nenana students ordered pins in the shape of Alaska—at a small cost (from Stewart Photo in Anchorage). Each student had 20 pins to give away during the trip to Europe. Students can keep journals, take photographs, and make videotapes to be shown to their community. Be sure to allot time for these activities.

6. *Follow-up.* Research demonstrates that students learn much more from out-of-school experiences if teachers create opportunities to reflect on them later in the classroom. It is the thinking about the trip that is most educational. Follow-up activities could include:

• Writing thank-you letters to people who hosted the group or helped fund the trip.

• Presenting a slide show or showing videotapes for the community.

• Presenting oral reports with visual supports, such as slides or tapes, to schoolmates, teachers, parents, and the local and district school boards.

Despite the expense involved, travel is one of the most valuable educational experiences you can organize with your students. Once they and their parents get behind the idea, you are on your way.

Variations

• *A trip to France:* In McGrath, Deane O'Dell helped organize a trip to France for all the students in the Iditarod District who were taking French in 1978. During the first three weeks of their stay, the students lived with French families and attended school. The last two weeks they toured the country—Marseille, Nice, Chamonix, Paris—relaxing on beaches, visiting fishing and mountain communities, walking through museums, and shopping.

• *A trip to the tribes:* In 1979, Francis Mitchell and 26 students from the Iditarod district embarked on a "Trip to the Tribes." After stopping at an Indian center in Seattle, the group rented three vans and took off for "Indian territory." Travelling from reservation to reservation, the students learned about various North American Indian cultures, including the Yakima in Washington and the Nez Pierce in Idaho.

• *A school travel club:* Students in Nenana worked for two years to raise the money for their month-long European tour in 1980. Thus was born the Nenana Travel Club. In addition to the first trip that included Spain, France, and

England, students have raised money to tour Belgium, the Netherlands, Germany, Austria, Switzerland, Lichtenstein, Italy, Greece, and Yugoslavia. When the threat of terrorism forced them to cancel their 1986 European tour, they headed east to Australia, New Zealand, and the Fiji Islands.

• *A senior tour of colleges and vocational schools:* Seniors from Kwigillingok visited community colleges, vocational centers, and universities in Seward, Anchorage, Palmer, Fairbanks, and Bethel. During their one-week tour, they also visited Kenai to see the impact of oil development on that area.

Students prepared by researching the institutions they would visit, mapping their trip, and learning the jargon of colleges, stores, and restaurants. Students developed a list of twenty questions that they must ask during their tour. They also kept journals. When they returned to Kwigillingok, they had conferences with their parents and the school counselor to discuss their career plans.

STUDENTS ACROSS ALASKA JOIN TO TRAVEL TO THE USSR

Karma Nelson, activities counselor at Juneau-Douglas High School, Alan Miller, Kenai teacher, and Rick Matiya, bilingual coordinator for the Kenai Peninsula, have something in common. They have led Alaska students through five or six Soviet cities for three weeks during the summer, participating in the American-Soviet Youth Exchange, part of the Initiative for Understanding. The program was initiated by President Dwight D. Eisenhower in 1956 to introduce American students to their counterparts in five or six cities in selected Soviet republics. Students are selected on the basis of character, their ability to represent Alaska to the nation and the world, and their desire for new experiences.

The 1989 Alaska group left Anchorage June 23 and returned July 18, visiting Moscow, Novosibirsk (a large city in Siberia), Sochi, Krasnodar, Riga, Leningrad, and Helsinki. During their travels, they explored the role of the U.S.S.R. in world affairs and observed firsthand the political and economic systems, cultural diversity, and ways of life of Soviet citizens of all ages. There are home visits. Interaction with Soviet teens is maximized during approximately three days at each site.

How To

For more information and applications contact the statewide coordinator at the American-Soviet Youth Exchange, P.O. Box F, Juneau, Alaska 99811-0500, (907) 465-2930. Submit application and letters of reference. Following selection by a screening panel, participants will be required to attend six two-hour workshops and one day-long workshop immediately prior to departure. The trip begins in late June and lasts approximately three weeks. The statewide coordinator works with the students on fund-raising, preparations for the workshops, and travel requirements such as passports and visas. Students and delegation leaders may earn ten university credits through the University of Eastern Washington. There is a student loan program which can help defray a portion of the costs.

Contact

Statewide Coordinator
American-Soviet Youth Exchange
P.O. Box F
Juneau, Alaska 99811-0500
(907) 465-2930

PART II

TAKE ADVANTAGE OF

STATE AND NATIONAL

PROGRAMS:

A DIRECTORY

In Part II, we feature the state and national programs rural teachers have found most useful for students in small schools. Most of these programs accomplish several different educational goals. We have tried, however, to classify them for you according to their primary educational function.

Benefits of Using State and National Programs

- Expanding the curriculum and teachers of a small school
- Tailoring the curriculum to individual students' needs
- Targeting new classroom materials to the Alaska environment
- Increasing students' competence outside the community
- Reaping the rewards of a tried and tested model
- Connecting yourself with highly professional educators

Cautions in Using State and National Programs

- Have a clear educational purpose: Don't use a program just because it's fun or handy.
- Many programs don't quite fit rural communities. Plan on tailoring the program to your situation.
- Keep in mind parents' worries about dangers to their children if they leave home.
- Be sure to prepare students for the experiences beforehand and help them reflect afterward. Talk to them about what they will experience. Ask them to keep diaries, give reports, and make displays.

Academic Enrichment Programs

■ The Arts

ARTISTS IN SCHOOLS PROGRAM

In Port Alexander, the artist-in-residence taught students and community members environmental design. By the end of his visit, students had designed their own playground, considering traffic patterns and what equipment went together. Students collected logs which had been washed up on shore. Parents helped them construct some of the larger equipment. The students are now raising the money needed to buy the hardware to put the more complicated pieces together.

If you would like to stimulate an interest in art or augment your art curriculum, your school can apply to the Artists in Schools Program of the Alaska State Council on the Arts. You can choose from two types of programs:

1. Structured program in which the school specifies the type of artist but leaves most of the hiring and coordination to the contractor, or

2. Independent program in which the school selects the artist and does most of the hiring and coordination. Under this program one or two artists are placed in the school from two to sixteen weeks, as the school decides. The artists divide their workdays into four hours of direct instruction and four hours of studio practice, when students and community members can observe and question them. Sponsor schools pay only a portion of the costs for each artist's residency. The cost depends on the number of artists, how many weeks they stay, and other factors.

You can choose from many different programs such as:

- Visual arts and crafts: painting, sculpture, drawing, printmaking, landscape design, leather, film, photography

- Literary arts: fiction writing, playwriting, poetry, journal writing

- Folk arts and traditional Native arts: carving, basketry, kayak building, quilting, Alaska Native music and dance

- Performing arts: ballet, ethnic dance, jazz, drama, mime, puppetry

DEBRA HALL

TODD PARIS

How To

Get an application from the private contractor hired by the Alaska State Council on the Arts to administer the program. Check with your district office to find out what procedure your district uses. Sometimes the school sends in the application and sometimes the school forwards the application to the district office for review and possible revision.

Contact

Jocylyn Young
Young & Associates
619 Warehouse Avenue, Suite 238
Anchorage, Alaska 99501
(907) 276-8844

ALASKA ARTS IN EDUCATION

Alaska Arts in Education (AAE) is an alliance of artists, teachers, administrators, and organizations that supports all the arts as a basic in education by initiating and disseminating quality art programs and resources throughout Alaska.

AAE is a component of the Education Program of the John F. Kennedy Center for the Performing Arts in Washington, D.C. Alaska joins Hawaii, Washington, Idaho, and Oregon as members of the northwest region. AAE believes that:

- The arts are basic to education and have inherent value because of the knowledge, skills, and values they impart.

- The arts and education community of Alaska should be committed to the improvement of the teaching of the arts in Alaska's schools.

- The preservation of the unique qualities of Native Alaskan cultures as well as the multicultural nature of Alaska's population should be a priority of its schools.

- Each child in Alaska deserves a quality, sequential arts education that includes cultural, historical, creative, and appreciative experiences as well as exposure to professional artists.

Contact

Fine Arts Specialist
Department of Education
P.O. Box F
Juneau, Alaska 99811-0500
(907) 465-2841

■ LANGUAGE ARTS

LANGUAGE ARTS PROGRAMS

The students at Andrew K. Demoski School in Nulato are participating in a reading program that has reached far beyond the boundaries of the school's walls. The program has been received so well that volunteers staff the summer reading lab, parents and older children read to the younger students, and 96% of the parents attend parent-teacher conferences. The village council has also endorsed the program and invested money to buy rewards for the students. The program has several different aspects that encourage a variety of language arts skills from the students.

The *Roaring Reading Rockets* is a program that rewards students for either being read to at home or for reading to themselves, depending on the grade level. As students began to earn rewards, the program gained momentum and more students participated.

The *Nulato Readers Theater* is also an integral part of the program. The theater allows students from each grade level to develop oral communication skills by reading their own or another author's work. Students then receive rewards and recognition for their efforts.

Noteworthy Features
- all grade levels take part in the program
- 110 minutes of language instruction are devoted to computers
- monthly school writing contests
- weekly schoolwide readers' theater
- rewards for home and summer reading
- frequent reading and writing labs

Contact

Principal
Andrew K. Demoski School
P.O. Box 65029
Nulato, Alaska 99756
(907) 898-2204

ALASKA STATE WRITING CONSORTIUM

The crux of the Alaska State Writing Consortium's revolutionary method is to place writing skills in context, rather than in a sterile world of abstraction. So successful is this method that former writing consortium teacher Paris Finley's students averaged two years of academic growth each school year verified both in standardized test scores and writing samples. Teachers rave about the writing consortium.

How To

Here is a brief summary, as outlined by Paris Finley:

1. *Identify a writing task.* Choose one that the students can get behind and identify with. This task can take a myriad of forms, from school papers to community profiles and church programs. The goal is to hook the students into some project they want to do.

2. *Focus on a specific topic for each of your writers.* Once they have a personal investment in the success of the whole project and know that it will be published and read, they are on their way to successful writing.

3. *Begin to work on individual writing skills that need improvement but only after students have begun to produce material.* Skills that need work will differ for each student, but error-free writing is not the goal. Published errors do not diminish the pride of accomplishment students get from seeing their names in print.

4. *Publish the students' work.* This should be the final stage of a writing project. A public display of skill and accomplishment serves to demystify published writing and allows students to learn to react to writing with a critical and appreciative eye.

Because the Alaska State Writing Consortium is growing in membership, you may well find a teacher in your district trained to provide in-services in the consortium's methods.

For thorough training, you may wish to take a summer institute course from the Alaska State Writing Consortium.

Contact

Language Arts Specialist
Office of Basic Education
Department of Education
P.O. Box F
Juneau, Alaska 99811
(907) 465-2841

Variations

- Glennallen High School has developed a project that produced a publication with historical significance and in the process taught the students how to use a Macintosh computer for creative writing. Area history was gathered as seen through the eyes of older people. For more information on this innovative method of using writing, contact Glennallen High School, General Delivery, Glennallen, Alaska 99588.

- Students in Anderson school have used writing as a means of researching the lives of their favorite authors and poets. Teacher Karen Stapf-Harris used the series *Junior Authors and Illustrators* to encourage her students to write letters to a writer or author commenting on a favorite book or asking pertinent questions. The students received responses from Dr. Seuss, Stephen King, Maurice Sendak, and Judith Viorst. Their most successful effort resulted in a letter from playwright Tim Kelly who gave the class an opportunity to produce the world premier performance of a new play, *Caribou Flapjack.* For more information, contact Karen

Stapf-Harris, Anderson School, Box 3120, Anderson, Alaska 99744, (907) 582-2700.

- *Kasigluk students write fictional biographies.* After discussing the wealth of black history acquired from reading *The Autobiography of Miss Jane Pittman* by Earnest J. Gaines, the tenth and eleventh grade English students at Akula Elitnaurvik in Kasigluk, Alaska, agreed that the history of their own Yup'ik Eskimo culture could also be captured in a similar format. Students set to work composing individual fictional autobiographies of Eskimo men and women. "This has been one writing assignment in which parents and grandparents have been tremendously involved," states Donna Murphy, a three-year veteran of the village school.

  The completed assignments were so professionally written and fascinating that Bain Robinson, the tenth-grade English teacher, put them into book form. The finished product, *Yuuciq: A Collection of Yupik Fictional Autobiographies*, is available for $7.50 each, plus $2.00 handling by writing to Yuuciq, Akula Elitnaurvik, Kasigluk, Alaska 99609. Checks should be made payable to "Akula Elitnaurvik."

- *Preschool research program stresses language and literature.* Nancy Karweit, a principal research scientist for Johns Hopkins University's Center for Research on Elementary and Middle Schools (CREMS), has developed a program that focuses on the development of oral language in the early years.

  The program, *Story Telling and Retelling*, or STaR, does just that. The program was piloted in a Baltimore elementary school in 1987 and is being used by 14 schools in Maryland, Pennsylvania, and South Carolina.

  "There is a keen interest in language approaches and in using literature in the classroom," said Karweit. STaR includes 100 stories, supplemental art, and suggestions for activities and sequences. Specific structures for the teacher's telling of the story and the children's retelling are also provided.

  The kit, which can be used by prekindergarten and kindergarten classes, costs $600 and is disseminated at the school level, usually through the library. About 10 class-rooms in the school can use the program at one time, said Karweit. For more information, call Karweit at CREMS, (301) 338-0814.

- *The Journal of Teaching Writing.* A semiannual publication founded in 1982, this journal is devoted to publishing articles that meet the needs of the classroom teacher and researcher. Topics include composition theory, cognitive development, revision, evaluation, business writing, creative writing, discourse analysis, curriculum development, and innovative teaching techniques. The editorial board welcomes manuscripts from educators on all academic levels and in all disciplines. Journal of Teaching Writing, Indiana University-Purdue University at Indianapolis, 425 Agnes Street, Indianapolis, IN 46202.

- *Experiment with Fiction* by Donald H. Graves. This book begins by showing how fiction is a natural genre for children. They like to tell stories; yet some of their stories lack cohesion, may be violent, and resemble play more than serious efforts. In this volume, Donald Graves helps teachers experiment with ten-minute fictional occasions, and meld work in writing fiction with reading programs. Heinemann, 70 Court St., Portsmouth, New Hampshire 03801.

- *Writing! The Continuing Guide to Written Communication.* Written by the Curriculum Innovations Group, this is a small magazine loaded with writing ideas and publishing options for students. A "teacher's edition" is given with each magazine. Writing! 4343 Equity Drive, P.O. Box 16600, Columbus, OH 43216, toll free (800) 999-7100.

National Council of Teachers of English

The National Council of Teachers of English (NCTE) is the national professional English education organization. NCTE publishes several professional journals.

Language Arts is for elementary teachers and teacher trainers who want to stimulate and encourage children to discover language—reading, writing, listening, and speaking—as a means of learning about the world and about themselves.

English Journal is a journal of ideas for English teachers in junior and senior high schools and middle schools. It presents information on the teaching of writing and reading, literature and language. It relates theory and research to classroom practice and reviews current materials of interest to English teachers, including books and electronic media.

College English is the professional journal for the college teacher-scholar. It publishes articles about literature, language, cultural theory, writing, and professional issues related to the teaching of English.

These three journals are published monthly, September through April.

Each year during the week preceding Thanksgiving the NCTE Annual Convention is held. Thousands of English and language arts teachers meet to discuss current issues affecting the profession. Through the program sessions, demonstrations, workshops, and study groups, members gain personal involvement, professional enrichment, and valuable information.

An annual membership includes voting membership in one NCTE section—elementary, secondary, or college—and a subscription to one journal—*Language Arts, English Journal,* or *College English.* Members also are given discounts of up to 30% on NCTE publications, copies of policy and position statements, discounts on conference registration fees, and regular member mailings including flyers about NCTE's most recent publications.

Contact

For information about membership in NCTE and for a copy of their current catalog of publications write:

NCTE Fulfillment Department
1111 Kenyon Road
Urbana, Ilinois 61801

Whole Language

Whole language is an approach that integrates reading, writing, listening, and speaking using real experiences in purposeful and meaningful context. It does not isolate or fragment skills, but connects language processes.

Written and spoken language is acquired naturally through repeated use in classrooms where teachers provide direction and guidance in a child-centered, literate environment. In the language arts classroom, children should be given the opportunity to read real literature (fiction and nonfiction) and to hear, speak, and write about it.

Marilyn Buckley of the University of Alaska Anchorage writes:

After 10–12 years of that focus (a decade of emphasis in education on isolated skills, "back to basics" and accountability), we're realizing that students don't have control over language even though they may know isolated skills. ... Twelve years of filling in the blanks doesn't prepare students to deal with the real world, and that's the impetus for this new direction.

Since whole language approaches are so appropriate for small rural schools, we include a more extensive description of available resources and materials. We appreciate the assistance of the Writing Institute teachers, who developed the following descriptions.

Recommended Whole Language Newsletters

The Whole Idea
19201 120th Avenue
Bothell, WA 98011
(800) 345-6073

Teachers Networking
Richard C. Owen Publishers
P.O. Box 585
Katonah, New York 10536
(914) 232-3903

Additional Resources

> Alaska State Writing Consortium
> Whole Language Resource Catalogue for Administrators
> Department of Education
> P.O. Box F
> Juneau, Alaska 99811-0500

Atwell, Nancie. (1987). *In the Middle.* Heinemann Educational Books, 70 Court Street, Portsmouth, New Hampshire 03801. "This book is filled with the details of conducting conferences in reading and writing, mini-lessons, working with various genres, the uses of time, grading, and proof-reading. Useful stuff, but still not the heart of the book. The power of the book is in the details of engagement between a teacher who has brought the full meaning of literacy into the lives of students—gangling, emotion-filled adolescents who confess they are too busy to read and lie about the numbers of books they've read in the past. Readers will see students deal with divorce and the deaths of parents, write letters to the editor, and struggle with what it means to be an emerging adult. Through dialogue journals Nancie Atwell writes some 2,000 entries to students extending them into new books, articles, or poems, all within the context of growing up. Her students gossip in journals to each other about the poetry and books they read. They speak, read, and write to live"–Donald Graves.

Baskwill, Jane, & Whitman, Paulette. (1986). *A Guide to Classroom Publishing.* Scholastic, 730 Broadway, New York, New York 10003. Children in a whole language classroom are writers. This book gives the teacher and parent lots of ideas of how to publish and display the works of students to promote sharing on a wider scale. As one of the Scholastic series, it is brief, yet informative, and covers big books to binding.

Calkins, Lucy McCormick. (1983). *Lessons From a Child.* Heinemann Educational Books, 70 Court Street, Portsmouth, New Hampshire 03801. In this story of one child's growth in writing, Lucy Calkins describes an approach to teaching writing that is already spreading to classrooms throughout the country. Calkins follows Susie from her introduction to the writing process through her early efforts at revision and at writing for real audiences, until she becomes a skilled and committed writer.

Calkins, Lucy McCormick. (1986). *The Art of Teaching Writing*. Heinemann Educational Books, 70 Court Street, Portsmouth, New Hampshire 03801. The book is widely encompassing, with chapters on poetry, fiction, and report writing and with extensive sections on reading-writing connections, writing development, and teacher-student conferences. Readers will find that the book is filled not only with workable suggestions but also with the faces and voices of teachers and of children, from kindergarten through junior high school, as they work in their classrooms.

Cohen, Alan S. (1988). *Tests: Marked for Life?* New York: Scholastic Educational Bright Idea Paperbacks. In this book the reader is asked to do some deep soul searching concerning the validity of Norm Referenced Standardized Tests and Criterion Referenced Tests. Both NRSTs and CRTs are brutally attacked by Cohen, with much historical explanation given to the chain of events in today's educational process of evaluation. Cohen's main point is that education should encourage learning and not turn it into a discriminating process. He advocates CRTs that approach education as a "never-ending search for instructional outcomes worth pursuing."

(1985). *Reading in Junior Classes With Guidelines to the Revised Ready to Read Series*. Wellington, New Zealand: Department of Education Wellington. Distributed by Richard C. Owen Publishers, P.O. Box 585, Katonah, New York 10536. Don't let the title of this book fool you: in New Zealand, junior classes are primary level. This book offers many suggestions to make reading child-centered and rewarding. It is helpful for the teacher who needs ideas on setting up a classroom environment conducive for reading and involving parents in the program. It has an excellent chapter on evaluation.

The handbook offers guidance to teachers on the use of the books in the revised and extended *Ready to Read* series, and describes the evolving New Zealand style for teaching reading in the early years. It also discusses the characteristics of skilled readers and teaching approaches which enable children to learn to read.

Farrell, Pamela B. (Ed.). *The High School Writing Center: Establishing and Maintaining One.* National Council of Teachers of English (NCTE), 1111 Kenyon Road, Urbana, Illinois 61801. This book offers guidelines for operating programs that provide individual help to student writers.

Gentry, J. Richard. (1987). *SPEL...is a Four-Letter Word.* Heinemann Educational Books, 70 Court Street, Portsmouth, New Hampshire 03801. Often spelling is taught in a way offensive to children. This creates a set of false dichotomies that prejudice children against spelling. This practical book demonstrates how children can learn to spell. It is devoted to helping teachers and parents to teach spelling as part of the reading-writing process.

Getting Started in Whole Language . . . Now Easier and Better! The Wright Group, 10949 Technology Place, San Diego, California 92127 (DWP0414). This "teacher-friendly" guide transforms whole language theory into effective practice. In it you'll find suggested activities and materials that will work in any classroom.

Goodman, Kenneth & Yetta, & Hood, Wendy J. (1989). *The Whole Language Evaluation Book.* Heinemann Educational Books, 70 Court Street, Portsmouth, New Hampshire 03801. The authors of this book—classroom teachers from all over North America, representing kindergarten through adult education—attempt to answer the questions of how whole language teachers evaluate their students. All of the ideas they present are proven, working methods of evaluation. Through descriptions of their classrooms and vignettes of their students, they demonstrate how they have created environments that facilitate whole language evaluation. They discuss the strategies they use in evaluating students' growth across many curricular areas, including reading, writing, and second language growth, and suggest alternatives to standardized tests in mainstream, resource, and special education programs.

Goodman, Ken. (1986). *What's Whole in Whole Language.* Heinemann Educational Books, 70 Court Street, Portsmouth, New Hampshire 03801. This book's major purpose is to describe the essence of the whole language movement—its basis, its features, and its future. It presents whole language perspective on literacy development, both reading and writing; it provides criteria that parents and teachers can use in helping children develop literacy; and it suggests directions for building whole language programs and transforming existing programs into whole language programs.

Graves, Donald H. (1983). *Writing: Teachers and Children at Work.* Heinemann Educational Books, 70 Court Street, Portsmouth, New Hampshire 03801. This book has become the basic text in the movement that established writing as a central part of literacy education and gave impetus to the whole language approach in classrooms. While many other excellent books have been published that elaborate upon and extend the field of writing education, none has had as significant an effect on the language arts curriculum. Graves' ideas have received attention from teachers, parents, administrators, publishers, and journalists, and his book has been reviewed, discussed, and dissected by educators worldwide.

This book was written to help both experienced and inexperienced teachers with children's writing. It presents no lists of what teachers ought to do. Rather it shows real teachers in the midst of helping children learn to express themselves: conferring with children, keeping records, talking to parents, and organizing the classroom. The book carries the reader through numerous classroom problems to successful solutions.

Hansen, Jane. (1987). *When Writers Read.* Heinemann Educational Books, 70 Court Street, Portsmouth, New Hampshire 03801. "I wrote this book because, since 1981, I've been a researcher in classrooms where teachers teach reading and writing more effectively than I did when I didn't let writing influence my reading instruction. The children in these classrooms read a lot, and both the teachers and the children look forward to reading. The teachers' instruction in both reading and writing is consistent with what they know about how children learn language.

"Primarily I wrote this book with teachers like myself in mind—teachers who have used traditional methods to teach reading even though we sensed something was missing. In addition, teachers who already give their students a lot of responsibility when they write will probably sense my urgency to give children more responsibility when they read. I also hope this book helps new teachers begin their careers with the understanding that authors' books are pieces of writing.

"When teachers read this book I hope that they will sense the excitement and joy of the children and teachers that I write about. I hope, in turn, that my readers will want to give their students opportunities to read, read, and read some more."

Hansen, Jane & Thomas, & Graves, Donald. (1985). *Breaking Ground: Teachers Relate Reading and Writing in the Elementary School.* Heinemann Educational Books, 70 Court Street, Portsmouth, New Hampshire 03801. Thirteen classroom teachers and seven teacher-educators break new ground on the important subject of the relationship between reading and writing. This new ground shows how process approaches in writing can be used successfully in the teaching of reading. Teachers have known for some time that children's writing and thinking improve as the children become involved in explaining their own writing processes from topic selection to finished draft. Twenty chapters from twenty contributors include primary teachers who show how writing and reading are used in content areas and who offer new insights into the relationship between the teaching of literature and writing.

Harste, Jerome C. *New Policy Guidelines for Reading: Connecting research and practice.* Available through NCTE.

This book suggests principles for evaluating and redesigning reading programs.

Johnson, Terry D., & Louis, Daphne R. (1988). *Literacy Through Literature*. Heinemann Educational Books, 70 Court Street, Portsmouth, New Hampshire 03801. The contents of this book include (1) underlying assumptions and practical teaching considerations, (2) initial instruction in literacy, (3) developing literacy, and (4) developing a curriculum. This is a highly recommended whole language book for using literature as a basis for the classroom language program. It stresses getting meaning from reading by presenting many strategies for the teacher of students aged 5 to 15.

Lynch, Priscilla. (1988). *Using Big Books and Predictable Books*. Scholastic-TAB Publications, 123 Newkirk Road, Richmond Hill, Ontario, Canada LL4C 3G5. This small book is jammed full of ideas for teachers who have never used or are just starting to use big books and predictable books as integral parts of their language arts program. Lynch covers everything from what to do the first day with a new book to analyzing the predictable patterns of a book. She concludes the book with a list of big books and predictable books from Scholastic and a short bibliography of related professional readings.

McVitty, Walter. (1986). *Getting it Together: Organizing the Reading-Writing Classroom*. PETA. This book deals with various aspects of classroom organization—topics such as the daily scheduling of the classroom, contracting, peer tutoring, and curriculum development. It also includes ideas for parents in the development of their child's literacy as well as team teaching suggestions.

Passages to Literature: Essays on Teaching in Australia, Canada, England, the United States, and Wales. Available through NCTE. Educators from five English-speaking countries advance new approaches to teaching literature.

Newman, Judith. (1985). *The Craft of Children's Writing*. Heinemann Educational Books, 70 Court Street, Portsmouth, New Hampshire 03801. The author provides a useful framework for looking at children's writing and examines case studies to illustrate how to understand a child's development over an extended period of time. The book is extremely useful for primary teachers and demonstrates the interconnectedness of intention, organization, experimentation, and orchestration. Recommended to help explain growth to parents.

Newman, Judith. (1985). *Whole Language Theory in Use.* Heinemann Educational Books, 70 Court Street, Portsmouth, New Hampshire 03801. Because "whole language" is not a kind of published program which can be purchased, Newman has edited various teachers' and researchers' practical applications after several years of observations and kid-watching. Her book discusses the most-often asked questions by teachers on the "how do yous" in whole language theory and curriculum. The text is highly readable and practical with motivational ideas that can also be of interest to parents.

Peetoom, Adrian. (1986). *Shared Reading: Safe Risks With Whole Books.* Scholastic-TAB Publications, 123 Newkirk Road, Richmond Hill, Ontario, Canada LL4C 3G5. This book is written primarily for teachers in grades two through six. It emphasizes the importance of sharing books with *all* students using "safety-netting" techniques for encouraging while reducing the feeling of failure among those students who are not yet ready to read independently. It identifies the needs and responses children face when beginning to read "chapter" books. The intent of this book is to help teachers build confidence in students as they tackle the task of becoming independent readers.

Smith, Frank. (1983). *Essays into Literacy.* Heinemann Educational Books, 70 Court Street, Portsmouth, New Hampshire 03801. This volume contains a number of Frank Smith's classic papers: "The Politics of Ignorance," "Twelve Easy Ways to Make Learning to Read Difficult," "Myths of Writing," and others from sources not always easily accessible. It also contains new material published for the first time and some "afterthoughts" in which he responds candidly to the questions and challenges he most frequently receives. They include, "Why are you so rude about teachers?" "What you say is impossible," "How can you teach a child who isn't interested?" "How will children learn if they are not continually corrected?" and "What would your ideal school be like?"

Weaver, Constance. (1988). *Reading Process and Practice.* Heinemann Educational Books, 70 Court Street, Portsmouth, New Hampshire 03801. This book is intended particularly for those with little or no prior study in the nature of the reading process. The author demonstrates that reading is an active process by which predicting, sampling, and confirming are part of the psycholinguistic nature of the reading process. Preservice as well as classroom teachers will find Weaver's book full of theory and practice for supporting the implementation of a whole language classroom. The book is divided into six chapters on the reading process and six chapters on the teaching of reading. It includes such topics as miscue analysis, teaching reading in the content area, assisting readers with special needs, schemas and transactions in the reading process, and ways to modify a basal reader lesson to encourage productive reading strategies and higher-level thinking.

FAIRBANKS WRITING PROJECT

The Fairbanks Writing Project, an offshoot of the National Writing Project, began in 1981 and now has trained hundreds of teachers in the Fairbanks North Star Borough School District. The Fairbanks Writing Project has offered courses in teacher training during the school year and in the summer institutes, offered parent workshops, and promoted a variety of student publications and activities. As a member of the Alaska State Writing Consortium, the Fairbanks Writing Project has been a leader in promoting excellence in writing in school districts across Alaska. The Fairbanks project, located in the hub of the Interior region, has hosted retreats for teachers and has been a

MIKE MATHERS

focal point for distribution of materials to surrounding towns and villages.

Writing is a means of learning. Along with the other language arts—reading, listening, and speaking—writing can serve as a means of sharing thoughts, ideas, and memories and become an enjoyable educational experience.

Once the student has achieved a degree of fluency (ability to put words on paper in a readable way), the teacher introduces various forms and models of effective writing. In order to achieve correctness, each student takes some of his or her writing through a series of steps involving rewriting and editing. Through the revision process, the student becomes aware of the need for correctness to ensure effective communication.

Analytical writing assessment is based on the idea that it is possible to define the components of good writing as well as to identify significant strengths and weaknesses. Specific elements of writing (i.e., ideas, content, organization, voice, grammar, and usage) are rated and then scored on an individual basis. The scoring device, called a rubric, is developed to include not only content, but also specific skills. Informal evaluation is also valued. Teachers continuously observe and record progress.

The Expressive is the newsletter of the Fairbanks Writing Project. You can get on the mailing list by writing to the Language Arts Curriculum Office at the Fairbanks North Star Borough School District, Box 1250, Fairbanks, Alaska 99707.

The following two articles are from *The Expressive*.

Primary Writing

by Bev Finstad
Third Grade Teacher
Nordale Elementary School
Fairbanks, Alaska
(907) 452-2696

Several weeks ago I was maintaining my daily vigil of respond-ing in my students' journals. Over a 20-minute period five different people came in to discuss something with me—five interruptions. The clock kept ticking, getting closer to the time I had to pick up my own children, but still I stood my ground over the journal tubs. A colleague next door who had witnessed these events commented, "Poor Bev, you've been trying to finish that for half an hour!"

She was right! Why not just quit? Because within that daily vigil lies the basis for a primary writing program. Journals can provide students with free topic writing, the opportunity to share, and the opportunity to receive a response. The teacher is given a daily opportunity to assess students' individual needs, the chance to model correctness and a chance to know students better. But these benefits occur only if the teacher maintains a regular dialogue.

In the same way a primary writers' workshop will only succeed if students are provided with the opportunity to write, to receive response, and to receive information on how to improve. Yes, primary students do need to make some corrections, but not corrections solely dictated from a teacher editor. Furthermore, not every piece needs to be edited.

I think most people agree that in the primary grades fluency comes first and foremost. Producing fluent, confident writers is our main goal. However, the question of correctness must be addressed. During the six years I've been involved in the Writing Project, I, like many others, have struggled to find my niche between the extremes of accepting everything and correcting everything. We have been caught between two ideas: one, that rewriting sometimes inhibits young writers and, two, that they won't learn if they don't see it corrected.

I feel I have found my niche by focusing on the students' needs. Students of varying ability and confidence levels need to be held accountable for different levels of correctness. An early stage writer should not be expected to produce as perfect a product as an advanced writer, even in things that are to be published.

Every student should make some improvements when publishing, but how many should be determined by their level of expertise. Concentrate on different developmental skills with each child. You won't be accepting "anything" nor will you be setting unrealistic demands. And, teach your students to help each other edit. Corrections the students find themselves are far more meaningful than those you find for them. You shouldn't be the classroom's only editor.

Linked Learning: An Interdisciplinary Model

by Diane Noble
English Teacher
West Valley High School
Fairbanks, Alaska
(907) 479-4221

Over the last couple of years, Sally Allison, in the social studies department, Dana Stratton, in art history, and I have developed an interdisciplinary model that we think works to help our students make connections between the diverse contents of the three subject areas we teach. The model has evolved into one usable by any collegial group willing to put forth the energy and commit the time necessary to make it work.

The model begins with several teachers, each with her own subject expertise, who come together in one or more brainstorming sessions. From these sessions emerge the ideas which become the basis for a unit theme. If colleagues come from a wide variety of backgrounds or teaching situations, some far ranging discussions might ensue before a concept broad enough and important enough to all could be agreed upon as the thematic center on which units could be based.

In this case these concepts become the basis for developing lessons and activities for content area units. Secondary teachers may be defensive about content areas, or have little time or energy to devote to the inclusion of a variety of subject matters in their teaching; the model serves as a way to build on teacher strengths, to enhance collegiality and to break down barriers between content areas, enabling students to perceive their schooling as a holistic, rather than as a fragmented experience.

The concepts developed from and with the theme serve as the organizing structures for the activities, lessons, and evaluations used in a given unit. Even though specific content may be different in various courses in which students are engaged, organizing structures for parallel units remain the same. A teacher responsible for several content areas should find such a model useful as it utilizes the same organizing structures for several subjects. A student may find himself looking at, reading about, or listening to the works of men and women representing the same thematic concept in art, literature, and music classes.

Most recently we worked in the American Romantic Era, 1800–1850. The unit's title, "Fulfilling Destiny," encompasses the three concepts the three of us chose to emphasize: the rise of an American spirit, the emphasis on nature and the natural world, and the importance of each individual member of society. All of us use this theme and these concepts when discussing the era with our students. Such reinforcement enhances their understanding of the importance of the concepts and also helps them connect the similarities and see the differences in visual and literary responses to the events and philosophies of the time. Though we organize our units chronologically, a thematic or topical approach might be the choice of other collegial groups.

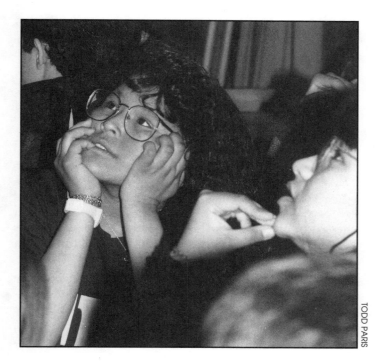

TODD PARIS

A variety of activities can be used to facilitate integration of content areas. Each of us has used various types including, but certainly not limited to, the following:

Synectics: Create metaphors describing an entire era: the art of a particular period, a particular school or trend in art or literature, a work of literature, the relationship of characters in a work of literature, contrasting economic forces at work within an era, or cause and effect relationships between historical events.

Write a response to a painting that reveals the singular emotion which touched you, that creates a biography of one of the characters in it, that describes the tactile qualities of one of the items in it, that captures dialogue between two of the characters in it perhaps in the form of a letter to the artist from an author who does or does not see his own views and attitudes reflected in the work, that describes it as typical or atypical of the era in which it was created, or that discusses its usefulness as a historical record.

Write a research paper on some little discussed aspect of an era: choose an artist, actor, or architect of a period and present a paper on him or her or perhaps resolve the conflict in a work of literature in a new way, taking into consideration the period in which it is set.

Make a time capsule for a particular era, either in writing or in representational form.

Go on a trip through a typical or atypical place during a particular era; narrate your visit.

Role play a historical event by creating a dialogue between an artist and a poet with similar or contrasting philosophies or between two (or more) characters from a work of literature in a situation NOT found in the work.

Create a visual image of some aspect of an era by using a variety of materials to represent such aspects as music, dance, economics, war and peace, women . . . images may be realistic or representational.

We feel that this teaching/learning model has benefits for students and for teachers and can be modified to fit a subject-organized educational institution and any curriculum model from thematic to chronological. It has made our professional lives better and has helped our students become more effective learners. It is a valuable addition to our instructional methods.

■ Mathematics

MathCounts

The new student had come to Eielson Junior/Senior High School in Fairbanks, Alaska, from a small, rural community. Socially withdrawn, she was an adequate, but not remarkable, student. When she heard about MATHCOUNTS at Eielson she joined with the attitude, "Well, I'll see." She met with the other members after school, but became so interested that she sought extra help from her math teacher during her homeroom and lunch periods.

The regional competition arrived. To her amazement, she took third place in the individual competition and first place in the masters round! Her success gave her the confidence she lacked. Even though she took no trophies in the state competition, she triumphed: she made friends, even with students who had come with other friends. She stayed until the end to see how her new friends would do. Others cheered her when she won a calculator. The competition is over, but she carries the calculator around with her and has worn her MATHCOUNTS T-shirt to church.

This remarkable change was the result of a program which does not, on the surface, sound terribly exciting. Seventh and eighth grade students meet after school to work on math problems. But the problems reach far beyond dry calculations. Formulated by the sponsoring National Society of Professional Engineers, they feature engineering situations. Some are real-life problems which encourage students to think about the future.

Participating students are known as "mathletes" to signify that they can gain recognition from math as well as sports. They work out practice problems after school or during math classes. The mathletes compete at three different levels: regional (February), state (March), and national (May, in Washington, D.C.) to determine who is "The King of the Equation."

How To

In late September or early October, each Alaska Society of Professional Engineers' Regional Coordinator sends out a packet of study materials, including drills, worksheets, and sample tests to each junior high school MATHCOUNTS coach.

MIKE MATHERS

Contact

> Clark Milne
> Alaska Society of Professional Engineers
> 1119 Coppet Street
> Fairbanks, Alaska 99709
> (907) 474-9580 (h)
> (907) 451-6009 (w)

National:

MATHCOUNTS
Camy Griffin, Executive Director
1420 King Street
Alexandria, VA 22314
(703) 684-2828

The Alaska Math Consortium strives to enhance the math skills of all Alaska students through exchange of successful classroom practices. Teachers from member districts participate in in-depth training which prepares them to lead efforts to enrich math programs in their school districts.

The Alaska Math Consortium is a collaborative effort between Alaska school districts, the University of Alaska, and the Department of Education. Each institution provides human and financial resources to support the consortium's training efforts. The Department of Education provides statewide coordination and promotes training opportunities and activities.

The objectives of the math consortium are to:

- Develop a positive attitude on the part of the student and teacher toward mathematics.

- Improve the quality of mathematics instruction at all levels.

- Retrain high quality teachers in mathematics content and instruction and upgrade their knowledge of mathematics.

- Develop teachers as leaders in order to disseminate ideas, techniques, and attitudes, and magnify the impact of the consortium.

- Provide training opportunities for minorities and women in the field of mathematics.

School year activities include AMC newsletters, instructional audioconferences, an annual meeting for first-year fellows, a migrant tutor training program, and a talent bank of consortium fellows for in-service facilitation.

Summer institutes are one of the primary statewide training activities of the consortium. Models for in-district efforts are shared during the institutes and taken back and implemented within the district.

The institute is a four-credit graduate mathematics course designed to strengthen teachers' understanding of math content and instructional practices. The use of problem solving and manipulatives provides the instructional basis for learning about geometry, probability, statistics and number theory, and other topics of current interest K–12. Participants share successful practices they have used in their own classrooms.

Interested participants from member districts must be selected by their school districts. Each member district may send a team of up to six participants. Participants should be teachers with experience teaching mathematics at any level of K–12 instruction. Participants must be endorsed by their districts.

All Alaska school districts, universities, and the Department of Education are eligible for membership in the consortium. Decisions governing the activities of the consortium are made by member institutions at an annual board meeting and through audioconferences. Member school districts carry out their own plans for strengthening math instruction based on, and supported by, the statewide efforts.

Alaska Math Consortium member school districts show their commitment to strengthen math education by:

- Writing a letter to the Alaska Math Consortium coordinator, committing the resources necessary to fully activate the consortium within the district.

- Designating one teacher and one administrator to serve as district representatives and key organizers of consortium efforts within the district and statewide.

- Working with institute fellows, district representatives, and school administrators to build a three- to five-year plan for in-district improvement of mathematics instruction.

- Providing release time for fellows to work on activities related to the plan.

Costs to member districts include:

- Annual membership fee.

- Travel and per diem expenses for district representatives, to attend a consortium board meeting.

- Stipend for a team of up to six teachers to attend a summer institute.

- Travel and per diem for consortium fellows to attend a follow-up training meeting for the year after their summer institute.

- Expenses for equipment and materials to implement instructional activities in the classroom at each site.

Contact

Alaska Department of Education
Division of Educational Program Support
P.O. Box F
Juneau, Alaska 99811
(907) 465-2841

MATH MANIPULATIVES

One of the newest revolutions in the field of mathematics is the use of manipulatives. Manipulatives are defined as physical objects that the students can handle, work with, or rearrange. The use of manipulatives allows teachers to teach abstract mathematical concepts using concrete objects. This translates into greater student learning and understanding.

Thirty-one students in Chiniak School are presently immersed in math manipulatives. This kindergarten through eighth grade school is geared to the use of manipulatives so that students can visualize math processes. Students are shown how to use manipulatives to teach themselves and progress at their own rate. The students work in an individually sequenced curriculum that is keyed to the district's math objectives and makes use of a variety of math manipulatives including number blocks, rods, cubes, squares, fraction bars, fraction tiles, decimal squares, and unifix cubes. The teachers also individualize the program further by visiting students' homes before the start of the school year to review past progress and outline present goals.

Contact

Chiniak School
P.O. Box 5529
Chiniak, Alaska 99615
(907) 486-8323

APPLIED MATHEMATICS

To increase student performance in mathematics, Boge Saffores' students participated in a self-contained, one-year course in applied mathematics. The students are required to have had two years of math instruction before they are eligible to participate.

The overall course includes materials that focus on arithmetic operations, problem-solving techniques, estimation skills, measurement skills, geometry, data handling, simple statistics, and the use of algebraic formulas to solve problems. The emphasis of the program is on the ability of a student to understand and apply functional mathematics to solve problems in the workplace.

Each unit consists of learning materials integrated into a learning package of supporting parts: video program, text, mathematics laboratory activities, and practical problem-solving exercises. Hands-on mathematics activity laboratories provide students with participatory experiences in the mathematics of the workplace.

"This program has proven a valuable addition to the math experience of my students," says Boge. "Their problem-solving skills have improved as well as their understanding of how they may encounter mathematics in their future."

Contact

Office of Adult and Vocational Education
State Department of Education
P.O. Box F
Juneau, Alaska 99811
(907) 465-4685

MIKE BELROSE

American Junior High Math Exam
American High School Math Exam

The purpose for these examinations is to increase interest in mathematics and to develop problem-solving ability through friendly competition. It is a competition that many teachers use as enrichment to their math programs, a fun and nonthreatening way to use math skills. Some teachers have ordered these materials, which are relatively cheap at about $12, and not entered the competition. Instead they have allowed students to work on the questions in groups and as a preparatory drill to other examinations.

The 25-question, 40-minute multiple-choice junior high test consists of a wide variety of math problems. The junior high exam, for students at eighth grade or below, contains questions related to such topics as integers, fractions and decimals, informal geometry, probability and statistics, and logical reasoning. The high-school exam, a 30-question, 90-minute exam, covers all high-school mathematics, excluding calculus. Solution sets and a summary of results are available to the school. Certificates and pins are awarded to top scorers. Past problem books and solution sets can be ordered if the teacher wants to make this competition an integral part of the curriculum.

Over 6,000 schools, or approximately 400,000 students, participated in the AHSME in 1988. Exam questions are available in Spanish and in large print for the visually handicapped.

Contact

Executive Director
American Mathematics Competitions
Department of Mathematics and Statistics
University of Nebraska
Lincoln, Nebraska 68588-0322

MATHEMATICS: ADDITIONAL RESOURCES

Alaska Council of Teachers of Mathematics

This organization is the state affiliate of the National Council of Teachers of Mathematics. The Alaska Council publishes a newsletter that keeps teachers informed about and involved in mathematics. Address inquiries to the association's president at:

Math Education Specialist
Department of Education
P.O. Box F
Juneau, Alaska 99811-0500

National Council of Teachers of Mathematics

This organization publishes a useful monthly journal that keeps teachers informed of opportunities and ideas in math.

National Council of Teachers of Mathematics
1906 Association Drive
Reston, Virginia 22091

■ Mathematics and Science

Young Astronaut Program

The kids are ready with their rockets. They have spent many arduous hours constructing them, beginning with simple kits and advancing to customized models. Each craft is evaluated for its quality of construction: seams are fingered, fins are eyed for alignment, engine mounts are gently wiggled to check fixity. Now is the test of truth—time for launch. This is the second part of the competition. The students crane their necks as they watch their work shoot into the sky. The winner is declared on the basis of the rocket's construction and altitude. The student beams.

The Model Rocket Unit is one of the packets students received as members of the Young Astronaut Program. This program aims to encourage students in elementary and junior high schools to study science, mathematics, technology, and related fields. Such packets as Physics Fun demonstrate the goals of the program: students study various physical forces and how they work on gyroscopes, roller-coasters, etc. Science and math are crucial factors in all space-related activities.

Because the Young Astronaut Program is financed by private corporations, each chapter is provided with $200 worth of materials for a $40 registration fee. Each member receives a membership card and certificate. In addition, every three months the school receives a packet that focuses on various aspects of space related to science and mathematics. One packet, for instance, has information on Halley's Comet, another on toys in space experiments. The students use the toys packet to study microgravity. They try to predict its effect on toys before they see the videotape of the astronauts performing the same experiments. A database is also available to the students. Accessed by an 800 telephone number, it is updated every month with current news of the space program and other monthly messages. Students can leave messages on the database to other chapters in the country.

MIKE MATHERS

The materials of the Young Astronaut Program, though written for elementary and junior high students, are appropriate for high-school students as well and can easily be incorporated into the math and science classroom.

How To

To establish a chapter, you must have a minimum of five members up to a maximum of 30 students. Individuals unsupported by a chapter can become satellite members for $10.

Contact

Young Astronaut Council 1211
Connecticut Avenue, Suite 800
Washington, D.C. 20036
(202) 682-1984

■ Science

ALASKA SCIENCE CONSORTIUM

The K–8 Alaska Science Consortium is a coalition of Alaskan educators and scientists working and learning together to improve the teaching of science. Consortium objectives are:

- to provide hands-on activities for the translation of science content into fun and exciting classroom lessons.

- to help teachers increase their own understanding of the concepts of ecology and physical and earth science, particularly as these concepts relate to the Alaskan environment.

- to help teachers learn science teaching methods that develop critical thinking and problem-solving skills.

- to strengthen the collaboration of teachers, school districts, the university, the state, and other appropriate agencies.

- to establish the mechanism for an ongoing, long-term training effort and to involve teachers in planning this training.

Consortium activities include:

- *Summer Institutes:* The month-long, four-credit basic institute is the primary training activity of the consortium. The faculty team of scientists, science educators, and lead teachers uses an integrated, activities-based approach to learning science content and process in both indoor and outdoor settings.

  Teachers who wish to apply to the summer institute must be nominated by member school districts and selected by the consortium advisory board. The consortium is looking for teachers who have demonstrated leadership and have a commitment to improve the teaching of science.

- *Advanced Institutes:* One-week, one-credit courses provide additional training in activities-based science and science content areas that are not dealt with in the basic institute.

- *Newsletter:* The newsletter, distributed three times a year, outlines new teaching ideas. It also reports on consortium activities and fellows.

- *Electronic Mail Networks:* Consortium fellows and instructors have access to the UACN computer network. This provides a mechanism for quick communication for questions, brainstorming, and professional interaction.

- *Kids Projects:* Students all over Alaska collect and compare data on a variety of scientific projects ranging from acid rain and snow to documenting the arrival times of birds in the spring.

- *Staff Development:* The consortium helps coordinate local, district, regional, and statewide staff development for member districts.

The National Science Foundation (NSF) is generously supporting the development of this consortium for the first three years. It paid the majority of program costs for the first year, April 1989–April 1990, and is decreasing its support in the second and third years as district and University of Alaska support is increased, so that by April 1992 the consortium will be self-supporting.

Membership responsibilities. The superintendent must:

1. Write a letter to the K–8 Alaska Science Consortium coordinator committing the resources necessary to fully implement consortium activities within the district.

2. Pay a membership fee of $1,000 per year.

3. Designate one teacher who has attended a basic institute and one administrator to serve as district representatives to the advisory board.

4. Allocate travel and per diem for the district representatives to attend the annual advisory board meeting.

5. Work with institute fellows and district administrators to build a three- to five-year plan for in-district improvement of science instruction.

6. Allocate $200 per basic institute fellow to purchase supplies.

MIKE BELROSE

7. Allocate travel and per diem for the basic institute fellow to attend one mandatory follow-up meeting the fall after training.

8. Allocate stipend for participants in the basic institute. This stipend is to be the district equivalent for participating in similar types of intensive training.

Contact

K–8 Alaska Science Consortium
Department of Education
University of Alaska
Fairbanks, Alaska 99775-0600
(907) 474-7341

ALASKA NATURAL RESOURCES AND OUTDOOR EDUCATION

In Nulato, students dropped sticks into the nearby Yukon and Nulato rivers and watched them float downstream—and this during class time! They were performing an inductive experiment. By measuring the time it took for the sticks to float to a predetermined point downstream, the students charted the speeds of the two rivers, compared the results, and speculated on the causes of the differences.

Around the river they studied rocks and land formations, took plaster casts of grizzly bear tracks (which had vanquished their plans for a picnic), and wrote Japanese poetry using the river as their theme. The river had provided an avenue for the precision of science and the imagination of poetry.

The Nulato students were participating in Alaska Sea/River Week, one of the member programs of a network known as Alaska Natural Resources and Outdoor Education (ANROE). ANROE links together such environmental education programs as Alaska Sea/River Week, Alaska Wildlife Week, Project WILD, CLASS Project, and Teach About Geese.

Although each program can be used separately, many teachers find that coordinating these programs provides a more comprehensive instructional unit on environmental science.

You can receive training on the objectives and activities of the ANROE programs by taking a one-credit course at the University of Alaska Fairbanks or by scheduling an in-service program or credit course at your school.

Contact

    Alaska Natural Resources and Outdoor Education (ANROE)
    P.O. Box 110536
    Anchorage, Alaska 99511-0536
or
    ANROE
    c/o U.S. Fish and Wildlife Service
    1011 E. Tudor Road
    Anchorage, Alaska 99503
    (907) 786-3351 or 786-3310

Alaska Sea/River Week is an interdisciplinary study and celebration of the sea or river coordinated by the University of Alaska Fairbanks Department of Education. The program consists of a series of curriculum guides augmented by teacher training and support services. Although aimed at elementary schoolers, the material is adaptable to high school and adult levels. The seven-volume set of books covers basic marine and wetland ecology and environmental issues. Each book contains background information and suggested activities, lists of needed materials, and a workbook section which you can photocopy for your students.

The program can be explored by a single class or by the entire school and community. Often, after one adventuresome teacher uses Alaska Sea/River Week successfully, the whole school decides to participate the next year.

The most effective programs have three parts:

1. Field trips to the beach or shore areas for direct observation and preliminary activities.

2. Community involvement. For example, have the students talk to the community's adults to learn the history of man's connection with the river and ocean. In Nulato, for instance, one resident told marvelous stories of experiences on the river before the times of outboard motorboats.

3. Interdisciplinary study. For example, for mathematics class students can perform scientific sampling and graphing by measuring all organisms in ten-foot squares progressively distanced from the shore. In English class, they might write precise descriptions or stories using the ocean or river as the setting. In physical education, four students link their arms together and run "octopus races" against the other groups. The focus of all the studies for the entire week is the sea or the river.

How To

To set up Alaska Sea/River Week in your class or school, you can purchase the books and proceed independently or you can arrange for an in-service. A complete set of books can be purchased for about $70 from the Alaska Sea Grant Program. To arrange for an in-service, you need to get district approval for the cost of flying the facilitator to your site.

Once you have district approval, contact the Department of Education at the University of Alaska Fairbanks. A facilitator will fly to your school to provide an in-service or a one-credit course. The workshop will include an introduction to the program, hands-on practice with both classroom and field trip activities, relevant science content, and suggestions for planning your Sea or River Week. Each in-service and Sea/River Week Program is oriented to the local environment. For example, the Sea/River Week in-service at Savoonga concentrated on whaling and walruses, while that at Venetie emphasized salmon and birds.

The in-service courses can concentrate exclusively on the Sea/River Week or include training in other wildlife curricula as well. The choice depends entirely upon your needs.

Contact

In-service:

Alaska Sea/River Week Program
Department of Education
University of Alaska Fairbanks
Fairbanks, Alaska 99775-0600
(907) 474-7341

Books:

Alaska Sea Grant Program
138 Irving II
University of Alaska Fairbanks
Fairbanks, Alaska 99775
(907) 474-7086

Which Alaskan wildlife are endangered species and why? If you and your students would like to know the answers to this question, take a look at the Alaska Wildlife Week educational materials. Alaska Wildlife Week is both a celebration of the variety and abundance of wildlife in Alaska and an opportunity to help students and teachers gain an understanding of wildlife conservation concepts. The unit on ecology, for instance, challenges students to look for and identify the interrelationships between living and nonliving things. The final sections of each unit ask students to apply their understanding of the concepts to real world questions and problems such as Why do some caribou-eating Alaskans have a high concentration of radioactive cesium in their bodies? What happens to wildlife populations when hunting regulations are ignored? What difference will it make to Alaskans if an estuary in Mexico is changed into a busy harbor?

The Alaska Wildlife Week project was begun by the Nongame Wildlife Program of the Game Division, Alaska Department of Fish and Game. Each year a thematic set of Alaska-specific educational materials on wildlife conservation is developed. Past volumes include "Be It Ever So Humble, There's No Place Like Habitat," on wildlife habitats; "Water, Wetlands and Wildlife," on the values of wetlands and conservation problems; "Wildlife for the Future," on wildlife populations, hunting, conservation, and endangered species; "We All Need Each Other: The Web of Life," on ecology and ecosystems; "Alaska's Forests, More Than Just Trees"; "Alaska's Living Tundra," on alpine and lowland tundra habitats; "Together, We Can Help Wildlife," and "Alaska Wildlife, Part of the Global Community."

Jerry Dixon of Shungnak School has used the wildlife packages for three years and has worked with students from the second through the twelfth grades. Here is his review:

> There is no upper or lower limit for this Wildlife Week. I have found something in it for each grade level. The program is carefully put together by biologists and educators. Units are planned and designed for the teacher.

Materials are accurate and concentrate on hands on activities. Students become very excited when given a chance to study wildlife. They gain insights when they play a game which teaches them about population fluctuations of the caribou herds and salmon on which they depend. ... In some of our courses Alaska Wildlife Week has been expanded to include a fortnight of activities. One particularly successful program has been noting spring bird arrivals. Through participation in this program the students have learned about different species of birds and their migration. It was students that correctly identified a golden eagle wintering in the northwest Arctic that has since been documented as a state record.

Since 1986, packets have been produced for three grade levels: primary (K–3), upper elementary (4–6), and junior/senior high school (7–12).

How To

For the past six years, the Alaska Department of Fish and Game has mailed the materials directly to the schools, addressed to the principal or contact teacher. The material is free. The number of packets sent to each school depends upon completing an evaluation of the materials.

Contact

Alaska Wildlife Week
Alaska Natural Resources and Outdoor Education (ANROE)
P.O. Box 110536
411 W Fourth Avenue, Suite 1A
Anchorage, Alaska 99511-0536

Wildlife Education Coordinator
Division of Wildlife Conservation
333 Raspberry Road
Anchorage, Alaska 99518
(907) 267-2241

PROJECT WILD

PROJECT WILD

When a large herd of musk oxen were imported into Talkeetna several years ago, science teacher Pam Randles pulled out Project WILD information on the behavior of musk oxen. Students learned how to observe the herd and came to know what movements to watch for and their significance. Project WILD aims to promote understanding of wildlife and management issues. Designed for kindergarten through twelfth grade, the information can be used in many ways.

When she taught at Shageluk, Pam used the "Know Your Legislation" activity. The nearby Innoko Wildlife Refuge was created by the 1980 Alaska National Interest Lands Act, which requires a public hearing on concerns and ideas on refuge management. In preparation for the Innoko Wildlife Refuge public hearing, Pam had her science students map the refuge location and study the possible conflicts between the different interest groups who used the land. Then in English class they brainstormed how the land could be used and wrote up their proposals, which they presented at the hearing.

How To

Information pamphlets on Project WILD are mailed directly to all Alaskan schools. If you wish to participate, you will need to take the required training course either through the one-credit course at the University of Alaska or through a six-hour workshop, which is free of charge. The workshop can be given at your school if you can gather enough interested participants.

The facilitator will provide an activities guide, including both classroom and outdoor activities, and will train you to use the materials effectively. The new aquatics Project WILD activity guide is now available.

Contact

Project WILD
Alaska Department of Fish and Game
P.O. Box 3-2000
Juneau, Alaska 99802
(907) 465-4190

CLASS PROJECT

CLASS Project stresses people's use of and impact on the environment. The program tackles six content areas: energy use, environmental issues (such as acid rain), watershed management, hazardous substances, wetlands, and wildlife habitat management. CLASS Project provides background information for teachers, posters, and specific classroom activities. Their publication *You Can Make It Happen,* for example, gives twelve examples of conservation projects students of all grade levels have undertaken.

If you have used CLASS Project before and found that some of the generalizations did not suit the Alaskan environment, then you'll be pleased with the newly revised materials. The wetlands program no longer discusses birds nesting in mangrove trees! CLASS Project sections on wetlands and wildlife habitat management have been "Alaskanized" and will include activities designed specifically for Alaskan students. Further "Alaskanization" of other topics is planned.

How To

CLASS Project materials are available free of charge to all teachers who complete training in the program. You can obtain training in two ways. Either you can attend the workshop closest to your community, or if you can interest enough teachers in the program, you can request that a facilitator come to present a workshop.

Contact

Project Coordinator (ANROE)
c/o U.S. Fish and Wildlife Service
1011 E Tudor Rd.
Anchorage, Alaska 99503
(907) 786-3351 or 786-3310

Kids Projects

Kids Projects are statewide networks of students in schools doing real research on a scientific topic. The projects are coordinated by Alaska Science Consortium teachers, and students share data over electronic mail or by regular mail. Students get excited about seeing data from other areas that are different than theirs. They learn to carefully investigate a scientific topic of interest. Projects continue over several years.

Donna Atoruk, a teacher in Kiana, will act as coordinator for one such project on ice formation on lakes, rivers, and oceans. She would like students to measure ice thickness monthly (after it is safe to do so) and also record the date ice goes out for a body of water that each school chooses. Gerry Young, a teacher in North Pole, has been coordinating a project that measures acid rain and snow. Data from this project is shared on a national level. Steve MacLean, the Science Consortium's UAF scientist representative to the advisory board, has offered to write up a project description for phenology projects. Phenology is the study of the timing of biological events. This will be sent to all consortium fellows. Steve has also volunteered to act as liaison between teachers and university scientists.

Contact

    K–8 Alaska Science Consortium
    University of Alaska
    Department of Education
    Fairbanks, Alaska 99775-0600
    (907) 474-7341

INVENTIONS

"Come on, show us how it works." The students are crowded around one of the inventions in the "Wacky" division. "Yeah, we want to see how the popcorn gets salted. Please?"

The shy, middle-school inventor gives his assent by pulling wires, winding string, and resetting the clock on his Rube Goldberg saltshaker made from Legos. The crowd waits, carefully watching the quick, sure movements of the thin young boy.

An imperceptible movement of his hand and the invention comes to life. A steel bearing rolls down an inclined track; a toy mouse is pulled toward a trap; the snapping mouse trap yanks a string; a catapult throws a marble into a funnel and drops the marble into one end of a balanced lever; the weight of the lever and marble cause the lever to drop, allowing salt to pour from the saltshaker onto the waiting bowl of popcorn.

The actions and reactions across the invention board are too fast for the crowd to follow. "Do it again! Do it again!" A faint smile appears on the shy boy's lips. He blushes with pride and resets his invention.

The Invention Convention in the Fairbanks North Star Borough was an offshoot of the invention section of the District Science Fair. Sue Yerian, who coordinated the Fairbanks Invention Convention, described how it began:

For the past six years I had been gathering materials and creating activities for an invention unit I present to my gifted/talented students each spring. The unit was very successful: well-liked by students and parents, highly motivating to participants and viewers, educationally sound in that problem solving and critical thinking were an integral part of the inventing process. We displayed our inventions at our school's Academic Fair, and soon other students outside my classes were asking if they could create inventions, too. It became apparent that every student would benefit from inventing, not just the gifted. Inventions attracted the high-risk student, the ones with poor motivation, the kids who wouldn't think of entering a science fair.

The Invention Convention had three categories of inventions: Useful, Wacky, and Display. Schools chose their top five inventions in the Useful and Wacky categories to send to the district competition. Any inventor could enter an invention in the Display category, a noncompetitive track. Prizes were awarded in each category. Wacky inventions include games, Rube Goldberg devices, and potential fads, among others.

As part of the inventing process, students brainstormed problems; found solutions to those problems; conducted research on similar inventions; chose one solution to the problem and created a working model of the invention; kept an inventor's notebook; and designed a backboard that explained the original problem, the materials used in the model, the procedure for operating the invention, and how well the invention solved the problem. Students had to "sell" their inventions (e.g., create slogans, flashy backboards, or advertise).

How To

Sue gave presentations on inventing to students in other Fairbanks schools and at the district in-services. A how-to booklet containing rules, judging criteria, lesson plans, and information on the national Invent America! competition is available.

Sue and the Invention Convention are on a hiatus as she completes graduate school out of state.

Contact

Sue Yerian, Coordinator

Invention Convention
c/o Education Department
University of Alaska Fairbanks
Fairbanks, Alaska 99775-0600
(907) 474-7341

SCIENCE: ADDITIONAL RESOURCES

Junior Engineering Technical Society (JETS)

JETS has chapters nationwide that promote exploring careers in the engineering fields, model-building, team competitions, and development of math and science opportunities. Competitions include TEAMS, where students compete on their high-school team in state competitions, which are held most often at colleges, universities, and engineering companies in their state. Then the first-place teams in each of eight competition divisions represent their state in the national competition, which is also held in each state. The top school team in each of the eight divisions will be named the national TEAMS champions.

Contact:

Junior Engineering Technical Society
(JETS, Inc.)
1420 King Street, Suite 405
Alexandria, Virginia 22314-2715

JETS also sponsors the National Engineering Aptitude Search (NEAS). The NEAS is a guidance-oriented examination for high-school students considering a career in engineering, mathematics, science, or technology.

National Youth Science Camp

The National Youth Science Camp (NYSC) is a three-week camp in West Virginia which is held yearly starting in early July. All expenses are paid. Its purpose is to acknowledge and further develop science leadership among outstanding high-school graduating seniors. Two students from each state attend. Participants are selected on the basis of their written proposals.

FAIRBANKS DAILY NEWS-MINER

Contact:

> National Youth Science Camp
> P.O. Box 3387
> Charleston, West Virginia 25333

High School Science Student Honors Program

The United States Department of Energy sponsors the High School Science Student Honors Program. Through this program students are placed in one of seven national research laboratories to work for two to four weeks.

Selection is competitive. Students are selected on the basis of applications which are available in the early spring. Seven students from Alaska can participate in the program each year.

Contact:

> Office of Energy Research
> United States Department of Energy
> Washington, D.C. 20585

■ **Social Studies**

Alaska Native Claims Settlement Act

Many rural teachers, regardless of their fields, find themselves teaching the Alaska Native Claims Settlement Act (ANCSA). This act fundamentally changed the political, economic, and cultural environment of Alaska, and shapes the future in which students will live.

Good curriculum materials on ANCSA have been hard to find. Here are some of the best and most recent sources.

1. *The Alaska Native Claims Act Multimedia Curriculum.*

These materials consist of four parts: videotapes for students, readings for students, a teacher's guide, and an in-service program for teachers. The curriculum was developed in 1986 by teacher Paul Ongtooguk at the Northwest Arctic School District and produced by the Office of Instructional Services at the Alaska Department of Education.

a. The Alaska Native Claims Settlement Act: An Instructional Series for High School Students. Five 15-minute videotapes on ANCSA, designed for grades 10–12.

b. Student Readings: a group of readings such as "Why the Natives of Alaska Have a Land Claim" by William Hensley and "One Day in the Life of a Native Chief Executive" by Byron Mallott.

c. Teacher's Guide: useful background material for teachers on ANCSA.

d. The Alaska Native Claims Settlement Act Teacher In-Service Program: five hour-long teacher in-service programs which concentrate on specific features of ANCSA. This series includes the videotapes for high-school students described above.

Teachers who want their own copies may order them from the Northwest Arctic School District Instructional Television Center, Box 51, Kotzebue, Alaska 99752.

The in-service and student videos may also be ordered from Media Services in Anchorage. Teachers in K–12 schools may borrow these materials or have them duplicated for use in the classroom if their school or district has subscribed to the Alaska State Library Film Service.

Contact

Alaska State Film Library
650 West International Airport Road
Anchorage, Alaska 99518
(907) 561-1132

2. *ANCSA: Caught in the Act (ASL order #96310)*

The Office of Instructional Services of the Alaska Department of Education is producing a series of high-school level materials through a contract with the Alaska Native Foundation. Directed by Caroll Hodge, the ANCSA Video Series will contain six 15-minute videotapes and a teacher's guide.

Paul Ongtooguk, a member of the Alaska Native Foundation's Review Board, said these two sets of video programs on ANCSA have been designed to complement each other. Used together, the two sets present a fairly comprehensive overview of ANCSA.

Contact

Alaska Native Foundation's video series is available and can be ordered from the Alaska State Film Library. Teacher's guides may be ordered from the Alaska Department of Education, Office of Instructional Services, P.O. Box F, Juneau, Alaska 99811.

3. *Books*

a. Robert Arnold's classic *Alaska Native Land Claims*, published by the Alaska Native Foundation, is still the basic textbook on ANCSA. However, it is out of print. Check with your school and regional libraries. If they do not have the book, then you can request it through interlibrary loan.

b. Smithsonian Institution's *Handbook of North American Indians* devotes Volume 5 to Arctic Native people. Besides clear explanations of the archaeology, history, and modernization of Alaska Natives, the volume includes an excellent thumbnail sketch of the ANCSA by Ernest Birch. Volume 5 of the handbook may be purchased through any bookstore.

c. As part of its ANCSA Video Project, the Alaska Native Foundation has developed a comprehensive resource guide. Prepared by Evelyn Tucker, the *Alaska Native Claims Settlement Act Resource Guide* reviews materials readily available to rural Alaska schools and includes nearly 50 pages of items on ANCSA. Chapters include "Curriculum

Resources," "Curricula in Progress," "Video and Film Resources," "Print Resources," and "Other Resources" (e.g., computer disks). The materials are briefly summarized, evaluated for level and effectiveness, and indexed by issues. You may want to send for this guide well before the school year begins so that you can send for the pertinent resources. Addresses and costs are given for nearly all the resources listed.

For a copy of the ANCSA Resource Guide, send to:

The Alaska Native Foundation
733 West Fourth Avenue, Suite 200
Anchorage, Alaska 99501
258-7452

d. Thomas R. Berger's *Village Journey* (New York: Hill & Wang, 1985) is a report on what effect ANCSA has had on Alaska's Native people. It has established a major frame of reference for the debate on the future of tribal institutions and Native corporations. *Village Journey* may be ordered from any bookstore.

ALASKA STATE MUSEUM LEARNING KITS

An Eskimo child examines the old-time whale harpoon and the *ulu* made out of stone. How old it looks next to the saw blade *ulus* he's familiar with. His great grandparents used such tools. He himself would have had he lived 100 years ago.

In an Eskimo village, children learn why black people have dark skin and curly hair and why white people have light skin and thin hair. Their world is no longer populated by just white folk and Natives. Instead, they see an earth of varied cultures which make people look, act, and think differently. They beat drums and pluck finger pianos from Africa and play with toys made for children on a South Seas island.

These are two of the exploratory adventures which Jerry Howard, coordinator for the Alaska State Museum Learning Kits

MIKE MATHERS

Program, brought to his students when he taught in the Lower Yukon School District. These artifacts—the whale harpoon, stone ulu, musical instruments, and toys—are parts of special kits constructed by the Alaska State Museum to teach Alaskan cultural heritage and cultural anthropology to rural Alaskan students.

The museum offers 62 kits in four major categories: Alaska Native history and culture, post-contact Alaska history, cross-cultural studies, and natural history of Alaska. Besides authentic artifacts (accompanied by proper handling instructions) from the museum collection, each kit contains various art activities, games, a videotape or audiotape (for example, the kit on northwest coast Indian art interviews elders and demonstrates totem pole carving techniques), and a teacher's manual suggesting lesson plans for using the kit. Though targeted toward upper elementary and middle school-aged children, the kits can easily be adapted for use with all age groups.

How To

To obtain a kit, find out who the contact person is in your school district. Each rural school library has a catalog describing the kits. You'll need to plan ahead, telling the contact person in the spring which kits you'll need for the following school year. The contact person will forward all requests to the museum, which will set up a schedule. The kits are shipped out in August and sent directly from one district to the next on the list. The average district loan period is three months. Kits are returned to the museum in May. There is no charge for the use of the kits; the district pays only for the library shipping rate and the postal insurance.

Publications that go with the kits are available without prior scheduling. The two-part mini-kit on Pacific Northwest coastal Indians is also available. One part is on the traditional whale house of the Tlingit culture and the other part is on northwest coast art with such material as bentwood boxes and explanations of how and why the people bent the wood.

Contact

    Coordinator in your school district
or

    Learning Kits Program Coordinator
Alaska State Museum
393 Whittier Streets
Juneau, Alaska 99801
(907) 465-2901

CLOSE-UP

Jo Dahl, former program director of Alaska Close-Up, was driving along, listening to Alaska Public Radio's broadcast of the Togiak Elders' Council meeting. She admired a very official-sounding testimony urging the members to think neutrally about the land in question, to consider it not in a Native or non-Native perspective but as "just there," owned, if by anyone, by the people. To Jo's surprise, the speaker was announced—not as the adult she expected—but as Jack Kanulie, Jr., a high-school junior who had attended the Alaska-Close-Up program in Juneau a few weeks before. Although he was not outspoken at the program, Jack had nevertheless gained the knowledge and confidence at Close Up to present his opinions succinctly and lucidly.

Alaska Close Up is a leadership program designed to increase students' understanding of government and involvement in public affairs. The year-long curriculum has two main parts: a week in Juneau to expose students to state government and classroom learning experiences within the home school. "It was the best high-school social studies activity I ever did with students," reports Bill Hatch, former St. Mary's social studies teacher.

In Juneau, students study first hand how state government works. They visit the Senate, House of Representatives, and legislative committees. They listen to state officials and other influential people talking about such topics as lobbying and the committee system. Students usually have breakfast with their legislators and explain to them an issue of local concern. They also participate in simulation activities, such as passing legislation in a mock legislature.

Teachers and students attending receive a study guide containing factual information on government, commentaries on public issues, and student activities showing how people actually can influence state and local government policy. Teachers help students complete the coursework and identify a local project: a community need or problem. This local project becomes the subject of research at home and in Juneau.

How To

Every September, Alaska Close-Up sends an invitation to every school district superintendent and high-school principal. If you are interested in having a few of your students participate in the program, contact your district office.

Prepare students for the program with the study guide. Help them become aware of political issues by reading newspapers. Set them to work identifying and investigating an issue of concern in their hometown. Organize methods through which they can check on the need, community interest, and feasibility of any proposed action.

Contact

Central office in your school district
or

Close-Up Program
c/o Alaska Dept of Education
P.O. Box F
Juneau, Alaska 99811
(907) 465-2841

FUTURE PROBLEM-SOLVING PROGRAM

"Eskimo students from Gambell win the national and international future problem-solving competitions." This headline was carried in an Associated Press wire to newspapers all over the United States. The problem Gambell students solved involved an aspect of genetic engineering.

The Future Problem-Solving Program (FPSP) is a program which teaches students to think creatively and analytically about complex problem situations. It teaches students to cooperate with others in a group to solve a problem and to communicate their ideas clearly in both writing and speech.

This is a national program sponsored by the Alaska Department of Education. Although originally intended for gifted students, it is now open to every student from kindergarten through twelfth grade.

Some schools use Future Problem-Solving as an after-school activity while other schools use it as part of classroom instruction. Students form teams according to age groups (Junior, fourth–sixth grade; Intermediate, seventh–ninth grade; Senior, tenth–twelfth grade). The primary division is K–3 and is not competitive. They register with the state FPSP coordinator and receive practice problems first and the competition problems later. Teachers show their students how to use brainstorming techniques, how to evaluate possible solutions to a problem, and how to do background research.

Students' problem solutions are sent to the state program for evaluation. Winning local teams travel to Anchorage for the state competition. State winners then compete on the national level.

How To

Discuss with administrators and other teachers whether Future Problem-Solving would benefit your students and how teams could be formed in your school.

Get program materials from the state's contractor. Some schools use these materials to teach problem solving in their curriculum without participating in the formal competitions.

Contact

Sara Hannan, director
Future Problem-Solving Program
c/o Alaska Management Technologies
369 S. Franklin Street, Suite 101
Juneau, Alaska 99801
(907) 586-4404

Alaska Geographic Alliance

On July 27, 1988, National Geographic Society President Gilbert M. Grosvenor warned at a National Press Club luncheon that Americans are lost on the planet Earth. Echoing the disconcerting statistics of a Gallup survey, Grosvenor informed the gathered press representatives and hence, the world, that of the adults questioned in the international survey, Americans scored among the bottom third in geographic knowledge. Seven Alaskan educators were among those sitting in the Washington, D.C., dining room who heard Grosvenor speak. They were determined to work to change those statistics in Alaska.

The Alaska Geographic Alliance (AGA) is a collaborative effort coordinated by the Alaska Department of Education and the University of Alaska Fairbanks. The goal of the AGA is to prepare Alaska's students (K–12) to function effectively in a global society through the development of geographic literacy. This preparation is accomplished through teacher training and curriculum development and improvement. The effort is funded with the financial support of the National Geographic Society and the Department of Education.

Teacher training for K–12 educators takes place at two-week summer institutes in Alaska. These intensive sessions feature academic geography instruction, teaching strategy workshops, and extensive fieldwork. Graduates of the institutes, AGA teacher consultants, are available for district in-services and conference presentations.

Curriculum support is provided in the form of materials and teacher-developed lesson plans. *Geoportraits*, a series of student-produced photographic presentations of community geography, are also available as models. The Alaska Map Project provides classroom maps for student and teacher use.

Communication among alliance members is through *The Alliance Reporter*, a newsletter published five times a year. The *Reporter* contains useful resources, lesson plans, and updates on AGA activities for the teacher interested in improving geography instruction.

How To

Membership in the AGA is activated by joining the Alaska Council for the Social Studies (ACSS), the professional social studies educator association. The dual membership entitles one to the membership privileges of ACSS including the ACSS newsletter. AGA teacher consultants are available statewide for district in-services by contacting the AGA coordinators.

Contact

Alaska Geographic Alliance
Department of Education
P.O. Box F
Juneau, Alaska 99811
(907) 465-2888

Alaska Geographic Alliance
Geography Department
University of Alaska Fairbanks
Fairbanks, Alaska 99775
(907) 474-7494

Also see Alaska Council for the Social Studies.

ALASKA LAW-RELATED EDUCATION PROGRAM

Research has shown that when it is properly taught, law-related education can reduce delinquency by increasing knowledge of law, encouraging positive behavior, reducing the use of violence to solve problems, improving school attitude, improving the likelihood of law-abiding behavior, and improving self image.

The Alaska Law-Related Education Program is a K–12 educational program that teaches laypersons about law, the legal system, and the fundamental principles and values on which our democratic system is based. It is education for citizenship in a constitutional democracy.

The program is coordinated by the Alaska Department of Education and the Alaska Bar Association with funding from the Office of Juvenile Justice and Delinquency Prevention and the National Bicentennial Commission. It creates networks of local teachers, attorneys, judges, magistrates, and law enforcement personnel and trains them to work together in the classroom. The program conducts training sessions and provides materials which reinforce teaching strategies that foster joint work among students.

Law-related education directories listing resource people have been developed in many larger communities and courses in law and contemporary issues have been developed for educators. Technical assistance and materials are available through the four national organizations that work with the state program:

American Bar Association/Youth Education for Citizenship
541 N Fairbanks Court
Chicago, Illinois 60611
Attention: Mabel McKinney-Browning
(312) 988-5731

Constitutional Rights Foundation (CRF)
P.O. Box 42815-281
Houston, Texas 77242

National Institute for Citizen Education in the Law (NICEL)
711 G Street SE
Washington, D.C. 20003
(202) 546-6644

Phi Alpha Delta Public Service Center (PAD)
7315 Wisconsin Ave. #325E
Bethesda, Maryland 20814
(301) 961-8985

How To

For further information on law-related education activities in the state and to become involved, contact one of the law-related education coordinators for the name of a steering committee member in your community. The statewide steering committee forms policy for the program and meets annually.

Contact

Alaska Law-Related Education Program
Department of Education
Marjorie Menzie
P.O. Box F
Juneau, Alaska 99811
(907) 465-2888

Alaska Law-Related Education Program
Alaska Bar Association
310 K Street, Suite 602
Anchorage, Alaska 99501
(907) 272-7469

ALASKA COUNCIL FOR THE SOCIAL STUDIES

The Alaska Council for the Social Studies (ACSS) is an association of rural and urban social studies educators and other professionals interested in advancing social studies education in Alaska. It is affiliated with the National Council for the Social Studies and the National Council for Geographic Education. The purpose of the council is to:

- promote an understanding and appreciation of the importance of social studies,
- improve social studies teaching in Alaska,
- foster unity among Alaska social studies teachers, and
- encourage research and sponsor publications related to social studies.

Members receive four issues a year of the ACSS newsletter, have an opportunity to share information and ideas with other educators at the annual conference, advocate for social studies through representation on the Department of Education's Curriculum Cabinet, and have opportunities for professional growth and recognition. Membership also provides automatic membership in the Alaska Geographic Alliance.

Contact

Alaska Council for the Social Studies
Brenda Campen
Box 1562
Sitka, Alaska 99835
(907) 966-2201
fax (907) 966-2442

NATIONAL COUNCIL FOR THE SOCIAL STUDIES

The National Council for the Social Studies (NCSS) is the national professional social studies educator association which currently represents 25,000 educators. NCSS provides a variety of membership benefits including:

- *Social Education,* NCSS's award-winning professional journal
- *The Social Studies Professional,* a periodic newspaper
- *Social Studies and the Young Learner,* a K–6 journal
- *Theory and Research in Social Education,* a research journal
- Educational and curriculum resources at reduced cost
- Networking and professional growth opportunities
- NCSS annual conference
- Legal assistance
- Travel and study opportunities
- Insurance
- Individual leadership opportunities

How To

Membership categories include regular, comprehensive, and student/retired categories. Contact the membership director for current rates.

Contact

Membership Director
National Council for the Social Studies
3501 Newark Street, NW
Washington, D.C. 20016

Joint Council on Economic Education

The Joint Council on Economic Education is a national nonprofit educational organization composed of representatives from business, education, labor, and government that seeks to promote the teaching of economics in the schools. The joint council publishes educational material including standardized tests in economics, curriculum guidelines for schools, and course guides for teachers. It also provides films, videos, and other materials. The joint council coordinates the activities of 50 state councils on economic education and over 225 college and university centers for economic education.

Contact:

> The Joint Council on Economic Education
> 432 Park Avenue S
> New York, New York 10016
> (213) 685-5499

Alaska Council on Economic Education

The Alaska Council on Economic Education is a nonprofit, nonpartisan educational organization whose purpose is to promote and improve the teaching of economics in Alaska public and private schools, kindergarten through high school.

The council sponsors economics courses for teachers, develops and distributes curriculum materials, consults with school districts on curriculum guidelines, and undertakes research on economics instruction. The council and the University of Alaska support Centers for Economic Education at the University of Alaska Anchorage and the University of Alaska Fairbanks.

Contact

> Center for Economic Education
> University of Alaska Anchorage
> 3211 Providence Drive
> Anchorage, Alaska 99508
> (907) 786-1901

or

Center for Economic Education
University of Alaska Fairbanks
104 Bunnell
Fairbanks, Alaska 99775-1070
(907) 474-6520

Adventures in the Alaska Economy

High-school students in Alaska are learning economics in a
new way—through an economic comic book developed by the
Alaska Center for Economic Education. The 100-page book,

ART BY JOHN D. DAWSON

entitled *Adventures in the Alaska Economy,* teaches economic concepts such as supply and demand, cost and economic incentives through the adventures of six fictional Alaskans: the Aleut, who leaves his home to hunt furs for Baranov and the Russians and works on a whaling ship; Ice Box Perry, who ships ice from Alaska and sells it in San Francisco; the one-paper kid, who seeks his fortune in the Klondike goldfields; Yin and Yang, two brothers who help develop Alaska's salmon industry and build the Alaska Railroad; and finally Dynamite Dinah, who blasts the Whittier tunnel and helps to build Alaska's infrastructure.

The book, which comes with a teacher's guide, was written by Steve Jackstadt, Director of the UAA Center for Economic Education, and Lee Huskey, Chairman of the UAA Economics Department, and illustrated by artist John Dawson. *Adventures in the Alaska Economy* is currently being sold to schools at cost.

Contact:

Center for Economic Education
University of Alaska Anchorage
3211 Providence Drive
Anchorage, Alaska 99508
(907) 786-1901

5

Interdisciplinary Programs

Just when you think you have exhausted your resources, you find a catalog of exemplary programs from the National Diffusion Network (NDN). Exemplary programs are those which have satisfactorily proven to the U.S. Department of Education's Joint Dissemination Review Panel that they effectively meet significant objectives. The NDN then disseminates information about those programs.

Whether you want a course on reading, science, vocational education, or physical education, whether you want one for the learning disabled or for the gifted, you'll find it in NDN's *Educational Programs That Work*.

Consider just a few examples:

Stones and Bones: A Laboratory Approach to the Study of Biology, Modern Science, and Anthropology. An innovative program designed to enrich life science, biology, and physical anthropology courses.

Critical Analysis and Thinking Skills (CATS). CATS is a program which offers students a sound, systematic, and practical way of analyzing issues and problems and practice in writing persuasive essays.

Law Education Goals and Learnings (LEGAL). A comprehensive law-related curriculum program designed to provide student understanding of the criminal justice system and of the civil justice system particularly as it relates to consumers.

Comprehensive School Math Program. A K–6 math program that applies math to new problem situations and uses various reasoning skills.

Whet your appetite? There are about 194 more programs! Just about whatever you want for your students, you'll find it in *Educational Programs That Work*.

How To

To find out more about these programs and for help in determining which would be most effective for your situation, contact the Alaska NDN facilitator.

Contact

National Diffusion Network
Alaska Department of Education
P.O. Box F
Juneau, Alaska 99811
(907) 465-2841

A COLLEGE SKILLS PREPARATION CLASS

In Kipnuk, both high-school seniors and community people enrolled for an evening course in effective study skills. Kuskokwim Campus provided the course materials and hired the school principal to teach the course. Each student in the class worked on an individualized program geared toward specific academic needs identified in a pretest. Principal Gene Hulse, who taught the course, said it was an excellent program. "Everyone who took it had an increase of one-half to three-quarters of a year in grade level." Several students who took the course went on to college.

Rural students attending college are often in for a shock. Coming from a small school, they may not have learned how to listen to a lecture and take notes. Suddenly they are confronted with lengthy reading assignments. To help students succeed in college, many rural high schools are now offering their students specific preparation in college skills. Students practice listening to lectures and taking notes, skimming through material, making outlines, taking tests, and writing research papers. They work with teachers on choosing a college and filling out applications and financial aid forms.

Some schools integrate these college preparation skills into their academic courses. Others prefer to emphasize these skills in a separate college or career preparation class.

Many of these college preparation courses include adults in the community as well as high-school students. Often the local branch campus will offer the course to both high-school students and adults.

Many districts have developed such college preparation courses. For one well-designed example, ask for the course outline of the College Prep Senior Seminar, North Slope Borough School District, Box 169, Barrow, Alaska 99723.

ACADEMIC DECATHLON

Holed up in a hotel with all the potential adventures of the city around them, the students study. They review mathematical formulas, practice speeches, and test each other on books. It does not matter that some are straight A students and some are C students. They work together toward one common goal—winning.

A scholastic prison camp with freedom as its prize? Hardly. These students are academic athletes, participating in the Academic Decathlon.

The Academic Decathlon is a national competition sponsored by private, nonprofit corporations. The philosophy of the Academic Decathlon is to encourage academic excellence in all students. The decathlon teams are composed of six high-school juniors and seniors (and three alternates), three of whom have an A average, three a B average, and two a C average or below. The competition has now been expanded to include students in the sixth, seventh, and eighth grade throughout Alaska.

The decathloners study academic areas in which they will be tested: mathematics, science, social science, economics, language arts, fine arts, and a "Super Quiz" on a special topic, such as immigration. School districts create a team to compete in the state competition that occurs in the later spring of each year.

Participants in the state's Academic Decathlon are awarded college scholarships to the University of Alaska and to several colleges in Hawaii, California, Oregon, and Colorado. Scholarships of $10,000 are awarded to the top ten highest scoring individuals.

How To

If you are interested in coaching a decathlon team, check with your principal. Your school should have received a letter from the Department of Education inviting your school to participate.

For an explanation of the Academic Decathlon, you may wish to view a 15-minute videotape on the program. Decathloners are provided with a study guide for each subject. It describes the areas to study, types of testing, and gives sample questions.

Contact

Alaska Decathlon Association
P.O. Box 301
Juneau, Alaska 99801
(907) 463-5812

It has arrived—finally!—the box the students have been waiting for. They tear it open excitedly and with gleaming eyes grab the treasure: BOOKS . . .

A teacher's fantasy? No—reality! Media Coordinator Alan McCurry has found just such enthusiasm for reading in the Yukon/Koyukuk School District. The motivator? The Battle of the Books.

Sponsored by the Alaska Association of School Librarians, the Battle of the Books is a statewide program to increase reading skills. Students participate at five levels: kindergarten through second grade, third and fourth grade, fifth and sixth grade, seventh and eighth grade, and ninth through twelfth grade.

The schools buy a set of books in late fall and students have until spring to read them. Then they start to compete, progressing from the school and district level to the state level. Each team (composed of three students) is quizzed on the books at its level.

All over Alaska, students use teleconferencing to compete with different schools. Alaska librarians compose the questions, which usually take the form of, "In what book did . . . ?"

Several rural school districts credit Battle of the Books with boosting students' reading levels significantly. Whether the teams win or not, Alan says, the students win because they read more books.

This is a competition where many small rural schools have competed against large urban schools and won!

How To

The Battle of the Books program sends each participating school practice questions. Teachers make use of the following suggestions to prepare their students for battle:

1. Have students divide into teams of friends. They are more likely to discuss the books with each other if they are friends.

2. Since many students are not avid readers, it is wise to divide the book list up between team members. That way, someone on the team has read each book.

3. Schedule classroom time for reading the battle books.

4. Design activities that increase students' comprehension of what they have read. Have them write out the book's dramatic form and act it out. Have students make up questions about the books and hold mock class battles.

Contact

For the name and address of the current Battle of the Books coordinator, contact:

Fairbanks North Star Borough School District
Library/Media Services
P.O. Box 1250
Fairbanks, Alaska 99707-1250
(907) 479-9410

DISTRICT ACADEMIC FESTIVALS

Yukon/Koyukuk School District

The spring festival is an extension of the regular classroom to initiate and implement a festival atmosphere where academic competition will flourish. Competition begins in the classroom where categories for the festival are filled with winners.

The annual Yukon-Koyukuk spring festival is a competition between students in the district from 11 different schools. The competition categories include spelling, superspell, math, super math, knowledge master, interpretation of speech, original speech, open speech, chess tournament, Native signing and dancing, and an open category for fine arts. Also added to the program is a fashion show for students to show their favorite dress-up wear and a science fair. Over 200 students participate in this annual event. Winners of events receive medals and certificates, and participants leave the festival with a learned sense of performing and creating in front of an audience.

Yukon Flats School District

Students from the 11 villages in the district assembled in Venetie to develop their writing abilities. They watched presentations on the theme of aviation to give them information and inspiration. Then they set to work. They wrote journals, created stories, and composed songs about airplanes and flying. They were rewarded with seeing their efforts in print. Their work was published in a brochure and placed on commercial flights to Fort Yukon.

This was the third annual Yukon Flats School District Young Author's Day. Based on the Alaska State Writing Project, Young Authors' Day provides young writers with a new theme on which they can hone their skills and the camaraderie of peers who share similar interests.

Academic festivals at the district level are growing in popularity. Some festivals, such as the annual spring competition in the Yukon/Koyukuk School District, allow students to exhibit knowledge or skills gained through a year of school. Other festivals, such as Yukon Flats Young Authors Day, help students improve particular skills in their areas of interest.

How To

1. Check with your district office to see if it has any established festival.

2. If it hasn't one as yet, consider hosting one yourself! Start small, so that it is manageable. Perhaps its success will stimulate such interest that the district school board will help organize it next year.

Contact

Many school districts have experience in organizing academic festivals. For one example, contact:

Dr. Nathan Kyle
Program Coordinator
Yukon/Koyukuk Schools
Nenana, Alaska 99760
(907) 832-5594

Knowledge Master Open

The Knowledge Master Open is a national competition available to elementary, middle school, junior high, and high-school students. There are two competitions, one in December and another in April. Schools that sign up are sent an Apple disk containing the questions and the rules for conducting the competition, both in a sealed envelope that may not be opened prior to the contest. The team size is limited only by the number of computer screens you are using and the number of students who are able to crowd around. The average team size is about 15.

Students answer 200 multiple-choice questions in a variety of academic areas, gaining maximum points if the questions are answered correctly within a certain time frame, and getting fewer points on a second guess. The questions are relevant to secondary curriculum in the following areas:

literature	earth science	English
health	physical science	geography
math	biological science	current events
government	American history	world history
art and music	economics and law	useless trivia

The competition must be completed within a 2 to 2½-hour block of time. Teachers may order practice disks (highly recommended) so that students may walk through the contest prior to the actual competition. In order to do well, students must cooperate, recognize each person's academic strengths, and know the material. For fun, get the school's teachers together to take the test after the students—see how the teachers compare!

In 1991, over 4,000 teams across the country participated in the Knowledge Master Open. Certificates are sent to all participants.

Contact

The Knowledge Master Open
Academic Hallmarks
P.O. Box 998
Durango, Colorado 81302
(800) 321-9218, (303) 247-8738

The Alaska Sister Schools Network was initiated in 1985 by the Alaska Department of Education and the University of Alaska Fairbanks to create opportunities for Alaskan students to experience more directly the cultural and economic perspectives of their Pacific Rim neighbors. As the education grapevine spread word of the network, overwhelming interest in the program developed. In addition to the Department of Education and the university, which are continuing to manage the network, many individuals representing the state's executive and legislative branches of government and private industry now contribute to the management and growth of the network.

The Alaska Sister Schools Network was launched by the public schools of Alaska and Hokkaido, Japan. To date, the major focus of the network has been on partnerships between Alaska schools and schools in Japan, the People's Republic of China, and Australia. Schools in New Zealand, Korea, the Philippines, and the Soviet Union have also joined the network. Although not nations of the Pacific Rim, one school in Norway and one in Greenland have become members of the 143-school network, as well.

Network organizers wish to go beyond the pen-pal approach. Specifically, the network encourages three levels of partnership: (1) initial acquaintance, correspondence (often by means of electronic mail), and exchange of materials; (2) curriculum development that focuses on the culture, language, and economies of partner countries; and (3) actual visits by students, staff members, and parents.

In some partnerships, teachers from both schools have decided to focus on a single project. In one southeastern Alaska junior high school, for example, the students created and assembled a quilt, with each square providing a lesson in Alaska history or geography. The students sent the quilt to their sister school in Japan with the agreement that something similar would be returned by the Japanese students.

In many schools, students have produced videotapes featuring the geography and scenery of their communities to trade with Asian counterparts. Short stories, poems, and artwork are

KAY VEAZEY

regularly exchanged. Students in one Alaska school estimate that they have forwarded more than 200 pounds of material to their Japanese counterparts during the last eight months. Food and everyday household articles also wing their way back and forth across the Pacific.

Network coordinators help individual schools in developing units of study by providing a regularly updated resource guide that includes general information on international communication, global education, and international exchange programs for students and teachers. Background articles for teachers, ideas for lesson plans, photocopied handouts for students, and news from the popular press—all of which are often difficult to find in remote Alaska villages—are included in the resource guide.

Joining the network is not difficult. When it receives an inquiry or request for information, the state department sends a simple application form to the interested school, asking for such basic information as whether the school is urban or rural, what the cultural background and language proficiency of the community is, and whether the community has any existing sister city affiliation. The application and other network materials have been translated into Asian languages for use in schools across the Pacific.

Project coordinators review the completed applications and select the best match for each school. The Alaska principal takes the lead in sending a formal letter of introduction and invitation to the principal of the partner school. Once the first round of diplomatic greetings between the administrators has taken place, classroom teachers and students take control.

The Alaska Sister Schools Network demonstrates the success that can be achieved when schools combine relevant curriculum with contemporary national, state, and community interests. Moreover, Alaska students are exploring their state's natural economic ties to other Pacific countries, so that these young people can take their places as the investors, consumers, and trade negotiators of the future.

Contact

> Sister Schools Coordinator
> Alaska Department of Education
> P.O. Box F
> Juneau, Alaska 99811
> (907) 465-2841

INTERNATIONAL EXCHANGE INFORMATION FOR BOTH TEACHERS AND STUDENTS

The Council on International Educational Exchange (CIEE) is a private, nonprofit membership organization. It was founded in 1947 by a small group of organizations interested in restoring student exchange after World War II. CIEE develops and administers a wide variety of study, work, and travel programs for Americans and international visitors at the secondary, undergraduate, and professional levels.

- CIEE offers a free monthly publication, *Campus Update,* to which submissions in the form of articles, book reviews, or letters to the editor are welcome.

- CIEE publishes the Student Travel Catalog, Work Abroad, and other information on CIEE programs. All are free and can be ordered from the publications department at the address below.

- To be placed on the mailing list contact the editors at the address listed below.

Contact

Council on International Educational Exchange
205 E 42nd Street
New York, New York 10017
(212) 661-1414

Japan Exchange and Teaching Program

The JET program seeks to promote mutual understanding between Japan and other countries and to foster international perspectives in Japan by promoting international exchange at local levels as well as by intensifying foreign language education in Japan. Eligible applicants must be U.S. citizens, under 35 years of age, and hold a bachelor's degree.

Contact

Consulate-General of Japan
550 W Seventh Avenue, Suite 701
Anchorage, Alaska 99501
(907) 279-8428
FAX (907) 279-9271

International Teaching Fellowship (ITF)

Alaskan teachers (K–12) may apply for an opportunity to exchange teaching positions for a year with teachers in Victoria and South Australia, Australia, through the International Teaching Fellowship (ITF). The program follows the Australia teaching year, January–December, and Alaskan applicants must have school board/superintendent approval to apply.

Selection is made by the Australian Ministry of Education and is based on availability of comparable teaching applicant situations in Australia. Candidates are given preference if they have:

- a minimum of 10 years of professional experience
- worked in a variety of situations

- recommendations from their principal or other professional colleagues
- evidence of a significant contribution to education, and
- their own residence.

The Alaska Department of Education also requires that applicants be willing to share their experience upon their return and review applications upon receipt by the department.

Applications are mailed to every school principal in September of each year with applications due in the department by December 15.

Contact

> Alaska State Department of Education
> Social Studies Curriculum Specialist
> P.O. Box F
> Juneau, Alaska 99811-0500
> (907) 465-2888

INTERNSHIPS AND FELLOWSHIPS

American schools are invited to host a visitor from Japan for three, six, or nine months. Offers study abroad programs for U.S. educators.

Contact

> Japanese School Internship Program
> International Internship Programs
> 652 Colman Building
> 811 First Avenue
> Seattle, Washington 98104
> (206) 623-5539
> FAX (206) 623-1702

Japan Institute for Social and Economic Affairs fellowships are given to 24 United States and Canadian social studies educators to help educators learn about contemporary Japanese society. These are all expense paid, specially designed 16-day visits to Japan. For information, contact the program coordinator.

Contact

> Keizai Koho Center Fellowships
> 4332 Fern Valley Road
> Medford, Oregon 97503
> (503) 535-4882

SUMMER INSTITUTE

The Consortium for Teaching Asia and the Pacific in the Schools offers a summer institute at the East-West Center in Honolulu, Hawaii. Teams of educators are invited to apply. Each team should consist of three to five educators whose participation would assist them in developing a strategy for improving teaching about Asia and the Pacific in the schools they represent.

The two-week institute will consist of lectures, curriculum demonstrations, field visits to resource organizations, audio-visual presentations, and discussion groups.

Contact

> Consortium for Teaching Asia and the Pacific
> East-West Center
> 1777 East-West Road
> Honolulu, Hawaii 96848
> (808) 944-7768
> fax (808) 944-7970

KAREN TENNESSEN

GLOBAL EDUCATION

Our planet's survival depends upon a dramatic improvement in global cooperation and understanding among the inhabitants of earth. Global education is one means of helping young people understand this fact. A number of state and national programs exist to help classroom teachers incorporate global education into their curricula.

The American Forum for Global Education is a private, nonpartisan, not-for-profit organization committed to preparing American youth for the challenges of national citizenship in a global age.

The forum publishes widely in the field of global education and offers direct technical assistance through a wide range of consultant services.

An annual membership will allow you to take advantage of the best of the forum's global and international education programs and publications. For a catalogue of publications and more information about the forum, write:

American Forum for Global Education
45 John Street, Suite 1200
New York, New York 10038
(212) 723-8606
See also Global Education Resources in Part III

EQUITY IN EDUCATION

Alaska's sex equity law, which prohibits sex discrimination in public school education, was passed by the Alaska Legislature in 1981. The law has been cited as one of the strongest state sex discrimination laws in the nation. This is in part due to the fact that the regulations require school districts to establish written procedures:

1. For the biennial training of certified personnel in the recognition of sex bias in instructional materials and in instructional techniques that may be used to overcome the effects of sex bias.

2. For the biennial training of guidance and counseling staff in the recognition of bias in counseling materials and in techniques that may be used to overcome the effects of sex bias.

3. For the review of textbooks and instructional materials for evidence of sex bias.

4. For the replacement or supplementation of materials that exhibit bias.

Module Series

Since 1986, educators within Alaska have developed modules relating directly to the curriculum content areas and the state's model curriculum guides. The modules were developed and written with the practical needs of educators in mind and are simple and direct in their format. The related readings and materials are included in each module.

Modules which are now available include:

- Women's History Month materials
- Alaska Women in the Fine Arts
- Alaska Women in Science and Social Studies
- Black Women in Alaska
- Alaska Native Women Leaders Pre-Statehood
- Women in World History
- Women in American History (elementary)
- Women in American History (secondary)
- Social Studies (4–6)
- Linguistic Bias (K–12)
- Science (K–12)
- Mathematics (elementary)
- Fine Arts (elementary)
- Foreign Languages
- Computer Equity
- Health
- Physical Education

Equity curriculum kits with teacher's guides:

- Teaching about Japan
- Teaching about the People's Republic of China
- Teaching about the Philippines
- Teaching about Australia

Modules have been distributed to each Alaska district and are available for a minimal printing charge, upon request.

For more information on this law and on all material, contact Sex Equity Coordinator, Alaska Department of Education, P.O. Box F, Juneau, Alaska 99811. (907) 465-2841.

PROMISING PRACTICES

The Promising Practices Program is a process which not only identifies model programs, but also recognizes programs that have reached a level of achievement that can be shared with others. It encourages Alaska educators to share their most successful solutions to providing the best education possible for students. The Department of Education has been committed to this process for the past 11 years.

Since the program was started in 1976 the department has brought together teams of leading education practitioners to establish criteria for excellence in 23 areas. Seventy-six programs in urban and rural school districts have been validated as Alaska Promising Practices.

Each year the Department of Education opens nominations to programs in the subject areas targeted that year under the statewide six-year curriculum review cycle. Programs that successfully complete the rigorous process of self-evaluation and Promising Practice validation are then recognized statewide for their achievement, and key factors of the programs are shared with other schools which can benefit from what those educators have learned.

In addition to Promising Practices, the Department of Education administers the MERITS (Many Educational Resource Ideas to Share) program that identifies and recognizes successful classroom activities and techniques that support a total school program. Established in 1981, the MERITS program awards a blue ribbon and certificate to recipients who are nominated by their superintendent. Over a hundred descriptions of these MERITS awards are published each spring in the

Alaska Education News as a means of sharing ideas with other educators.

Contact

For further information on Promising Practices or the MERITS program contact:

Office of Basic Education
Department of Education
P.O. Box F
Juneau, Alaska 99811
(907) 465-2644

6

Correspondence Study Programs

When considering how to expand the curriculum, don't forget that old stand-by, correspondence study. You can use these courses to cover subjects that you don't have the background to teach or to offer advanced work for a small number of students.

Many school districts offer their own correspondence programs. We list below the three correspondence programs most commonly used in Alaska. If they don't offer the course you need, the staff can usually tell you what program does offer it.

CENTRALIZED CORRESPONDENCE STUDY

Centralized Correspondence Study (CCS) is a program run by the Alaska Department of Education. Though increasingly developing its own courses, at this time it still purchases some of its high-school courses from a variety of established correspondence schools. It is fully accredited by the Northwest Association of Schools and Colleges.

CENTER FOR CROSS-CULTURAL STUDIES

   Your district has two options in using CCS. Both allow it to offer academically solid courses to students without teachers certified or endorsed in those fields.

   Option 1: You can purchase the course materials only and use a local teacher to teach and monitor the students.

   Option 2: You can purchase CCS's teaching service, which includes scheduling the assignments, diagnosing student needs, and grading the tests, along with course materials.

CCS teachers hold Alaska teaching certificates endorsed in the field and have classroom experience.

Contact

Tantamount is district approval. Once that is obtained, you can request a catalog of courses and complete information on policies from:

Centralized Correspondence Study
Box GA
Juneau, Alaska 99811
(907) 465-2835

University of Nebraska–Lincoln Independent Study High School

In existence in the early 1920s, the University of Nebraska–Lincoln Independent Study High School is one of the largest university-based correspondence study programs in the United States.

UNL offers 123 courses for grades 9–12. It is fully accredited by the North Central Association of Colleges and Schools.

As with Alaska Centralized Correspondence Study, the University of Nebraska allows you two options of offering their programs to the students in your classes:

Option 1: You can purchase the course materials only (syllabi and curriculum guides, including discussion questions, worksheets, self-check tests, and tests), and teach and monitor the students locally.

Option 2: You can enroll students with the University of Nebraska–Lincoln Independent Study High School and use their teachers to evaluate the tests and worksheets and award credit.

Contact

For complete policies and a catalog of courses, write to:

Independent Study High School
Division of Continuing Studies
Nebraska Center for Continuing Education
33rd and Holdrege Streets
University of Nebraska–Lincoln
Lincoln, Nebraska 68583-0900
(402) 472-1926

UNIVERSITY OF ALASKA CORRESPONDENCE STUDY PROGRAM

High-school students with the interest and ability to complete college level courses can enroll in the University of Alaska's correspondence program. The courses, accredited through the University of Alaska, are substantially the same in content and scope as those taught on campus.

Teachers can enroll and apply three of these correspondence credits toward the six credits required by the Alaska Department of Education for teacher recertification.

In addition to standard courses, correspondence study offers many courses specific to Alaska, such as Elementary Inupiaq and Geography of Alaska. Correspondence study is a member of the National University Continuing Education Association and will help you find courses you need offered by other universities.

Contact

Center for Distance Education
College of Rural Alaska
Room 130 Red Building
University of Alaska Fairbanks
Fairbanks, Alaska 99775-0560
(907) 474-7222

See Also

If you would like a complete listing of the correspondence courses offered by members of the National University Continuing Education Association (NUCEA), you can purchase their catalog, Peterson's Guide, by writing to:

NUCEA Book Order Department
Peterson's Guide
P.O. Box 2123
Princeton, New Jersey 08540-2123
(609) 243-9111

Practical Skills Programs

■ Work Experience

A young deaf man who was taking a welding course in his high school in Galena was accepted into the Rural Student Vocational Program (RSVP) to work as a welder at Ft. Wainwright. As part of his RSVP experience, he worked with the state Division of Vocational Rehabilitation, learning how to live independently. He successfully completed the program and is now living on his own in Fairbanks. His occupation? Welding.

RSVP is a widely known state program that accomplishes two goals: to give students work experience (especially in a field of career interest) and to familiarize them with urban living.

All juniors and seniors enrolled in vocational education programs in their schools are eligible for RSVP. Those interested in the program can apply by filling out a form that resembles a formal job application and also a vocational interest form.

Regional RSVP coordinators place students in work situations—business, carpentry, data processing, health care, or industry.

When the students arrive in Anchorage, Fairbanks, or Juneau (the Alaska RSVP sites), they are given an orientation which includes rules, work site and boarding home information, career exploration, and urban survival information. For two weeks they work at the job site. They live with urban families who provide a cross-cultural living experience.

DAVE STONE

How To

Initial Contact: Each fall the regional coordinator mails to the principal or the previous RSVP contact teacher a packet containing information on work sites, guidelines for student selection and preparation, and student applications.

Preparation: The RSVP experience is much more profitable if you match students with jobs in which they have an interest.

Yukon Flats School District, for example, uses three devices to identify career interests:

1. Interest Determination Exploration and Assessment System (IDEAS)

2. Career Assessment Inventory

Both can be obtained from National Computer Systems, 5605 Green Circle Drive, Minnetonka, Minnesota 55343, (612) 933-2800 or (800) 328-6759 (toll free number).

Follow-Up: Research shows that students need to reflect on experiences outside the classroom if they are to learn from them. Ask students to keep diaries, write a short story about first experiences, or make presentations on their trip.

Contact

For the name of the RSVP coordinator in your region, contact:

Program Manager
Office of Adult Vocational Education
Alaska Department of Education
P.O. Box F
Juneau, Alaska 99811
(907) 465-4685

■ **Student Organizations**

VOCATIONAL STUDENT LEADERSHIP ORGANIZATIONS

All year, June Hyska coached her 15 Nunapitchuk students, members of the Vocational Industrial Clubs of America (VICA) Leadership Program, in the goals of the program and parliamentary procedure. Interest remained high until the meetings began to conflict with ball games and the statewide competition neared. Then students wanted to trade their hard work and nervousness for more obvious fun. But June wouldn't let them. She threatened not to take them to the state conference if they were going to embarrass her and themselves with a poor performance. She told the team they couldn't back out.

The Nunapitchuk students won the state championship even though English is their second language.

They sang "My Old Kentucky Home" all the way to the national VICA competition in Louisville, Kentucky. There they found 7,000 other students who were intrigued and thrilled with these Eskimo contestants from a school of 30. June's students swept the national VICA competition and received a standing ovation from the state directors when they presented the opening and closing ceremonies in Yup'ik.

The VICA program in which the Nunapitchuk students participated is one of the nationwide Vocational Student Leadership Organizations. These include:

- Future Farmers of America (FFA)
- Distributive Education Clubs of America (DECA)
- Office Education Association (OEA)
- Future Homemakers of America/Home Economics Related Occupations (FHA/HERO)
- Vocational Industrial Clubs of America (VICA)

All groups of the Vocational Student Leadership Organization have the same primary objective: to introduce students to the essentials of a particular vocation and to sharpen the appropriate technical and social skills. Secondary objectives include developing leadership through formal, structured business meetings, fostering citizenship through school and community service projects, providing business experience through fund-raising activities, and organizing social and recreational opportunities between people with similar interests.

How To

Because it is sometimes difficult in rural areas to get enough members to form a chapter for each organization, the vocational education equity manager suggests that the assorted members affiliate with a nearby Vocational Student Leadership Organization chapter.

Contact

Leadership Experiences International
610C W 47th Avenue
Anchorage, Alaska 99503
(907) 563-7882
fax (907) 563-7434
or

Program Manager
Student Leadership Project Office of Adult Vocational Education
Alaska Department of Education
P.O. Box F
Juneau, Alaska 99811
(907) 465-4685

Variation

Students in Akiachak have used their vocational education skills not only to further their own knowledge but also to build good community relations and to further their job possibilities after graduation.

Francis Schneider used his Vocational Education class to teach students about welding, furniture construction, and house construction. Students participated in projects including the construction of an all welded aluminum freight sled, a useful product and one that was fun to make.

Contact

For further information on this Alaska teacher's ideas and methods, contact:

Akiachak High School
General Delivery
Akiachak, Alaska 99551
(907) 825-4013

STUDENT LEADERSHIP ORGANIZATIONS AND THE STUDENT LEADERSHIP PROJECT

A Student Leadership Organization (SLO) provides learning experiences to help students develop leadership, citizenship, and social skills. Through these organizations, students can develop attitudes and acquire knowledge and skills that are essential to success in both personal and professional life. These organizations benefit students by providing opportunities to become involved in public speaking, communications, problem solving, and parliamentary procedure, to learn to work as part of a team, and to develop a sense of self worth and pride.

SLOs benefit teachers by providing opportunities to motivate and challenge students through SLO activities, to better know and understand students, and to see students successfully apply skills learned in the classroom. The overall school program is enhanced by SLOs because they provide opportunities to develop leadership skills that help students to become knowledgeable participants in the community. SLOs can also involve parents and other community members in student programs.

The purpose of the Student Leadership Project is to help Alaska's secondary school students to develop leadership skills. Project staff work primarily with the state advisors, officers, and members of Alaska's SLOs, but project activities are also available to students who are not members of those organizations. The Student Leadership Project seeks to:

- provide leadership workshops for students in school districts requesting such training

- conduct SLO state officer training in leadership and organizational planning

- give assistance to SLOs in strengthening and expanding their organizations

- award block grant funds to each SLO which enable it to carry out its annual program of work

One of the main objectives of the project is to provide leadership training for secondary students throughout Alaska. Workshops are conducted to teach such skills as parliamentary procedure, public speaking, group problem solving, and goal setting. Project staff, state advisors, and SLO state officers travel to local communities to conduct these workshops. Since the beginning of the project in 1980, leadership workshops have involved students in over 120 secondary schools.

Another goal is to provide training for the state officers of the SLOs involved in the project. Training sessions are presented in order to help state officers conduct local leadership workshops. In the spring, officers meet in Juneau where they have the opportunity to talk with legislators and learn how Alaska's government operates.

In order to strengthen the skill-building capability of the six SLOs involved in the project, funds are provided in several areas. Contracts are written to provide for the services of each SLO's state advisor. Project staff at Leadership Experiences International are also available to assist in planning and conducting state conferences.

Grant funds are provided to strengthen and expand SLOs. The state advisor and state officers of each SLO develop a program of work that outlines how its grant funds are spent. Block grant funds are used for activities such as SLO newsletters, state conferences, and chapter handbooks.

Six SLOs participate in the Student Leadership Project:

Alaska Association of School Governments (AASG) is the statewide organization for members of student councils in all of Alaska's secondary schools.

Distributive Education Clubs of America (DECA) is an organization for secondary school students preparing for careers in marketing, merchandising, and management.

Future Farmers of America (FFA) is an organization for students preparing for careers on the farm, in agribusinesses that support farmers, and in the fields of forestry, horticulture, food processing, and natural resources.

Future Homemakers of America (FHA) is an organization for students seeking to improve personal, family, and community living through home economics and related courses.

Business Professionals of America (BPA) is an organization designed to develop leadership abilities, competency in office skills, and interest in the American business system.

Vocational Industrial Clubs of America (VICA) is an organization for students enrolled in trade, industrial technical, and health occupations programs in secondary and postsecondary schools.

Contact

Office of Adult and Vocational Education
Department of Education
P.O. Box F
Juneau, Alaska 99811-0500
(907) 465-4685

or

Leadership Experiences International
610C W 47th Avenue
Anchorage, Alaska 99503
(907) 563-7882
fax (907) 563-7434

■ **Help for Parents**

THE EARLY ADOLESCENT HELPER PROGRAM

Marie, a high-school junior, snuggled three-year-old Tommy and read from Jean Rogers' new Alaska picture book. Marie was working in the community Head Start program as part of her home economics course. She had learned that reading to preschool children is the most important thing you can do to develop positive attitudes toward reading.

The Early Adolescent Helper Program places young teenagers (11–15 years old) as interns in community agencies. One of the most successful projects of the Helper Program and that most applicable to Alaska is the Early Adolescent Child Care

DAVE STONE

Helper Project, which trains students to work in a local child care or Head Start center.

The project, usually integrated into the curriculum, has two parts: (1) an in-school seminar in which students study such issues as child development, child care, discipline, problem solving, parenting, and self-assessment; and (2) work experience at the child care site. Also, there is the requirement of a time for reflection for the helpers that is built into the structure of the program. This time enables students to think back on their service experience while it is still fresh in their minds, share their concerns about their work, and collaborate with the group to find solutions to any problems they may have encountered.

Many teens gain immense self-respect when they see someone blossom under their care. The transformation is especially evident in youth who come from abusing families, who learn that they can discipline a misbehaving child in a calm and effective manner.

How To

You can purchase the *Child Care Helper Program: A Guide for Teachers and Program Leaders* for $15.

Here are some useful suggestions for running an effective program:

1. Recruit helpers by showing your young students what they can do for those who are younger than they are. Use concrete examples and photographs. Once you have captured their interest, make them aware that they are making a commitment to the children and they cannot arbitrarily drop out of the program.

2. Negotiate a written "contract" to which the school, helpers, and child-care center or parents of the children involved all agree. Signing the contract will clarify the goals of the program and reinforce to the helpers the depth of their commitment.

3. Have students keep journals about their experiences. These can form the base for stories in English class or discussions in health or psychology class.

4. Have other students make videotapes of the helpers at work in the child care center. Then have the helpers present a program for other students and community members of the work they do and the experiences they have had.

5. Reward the helpers often and in creative ways: certificates from the mayor's office, T-shirts, and parties are all effective. Mainly, show them that they are appreciated and respected.

The Partners Program is designed to bring together two groups of people—young adolescents and senior citizens—who have much to learn from each other, but who do not ordinarily have the opportunity to spend time together in a supportive and positive setting.

It enables students to have an opportunity to learn about their community from the rich perspective of seniors who can talk about changes they have witnessed and to offer senior citizens an opportunity to influence the future of the community through its young men and women.

The Partners Program challenges the young adolescent to discover and test new skills, to build new relationships, and to develop a sense of competence. The seminar and on-site work experience complement each other, and help students make the connection between classroom learning and the "real world."

Contact for both Partners Program and Early Adolecent Helper Program:

National Center for Service Learning
CASE: CUNY Graduate Center
25 W 43rd Street, Suite 612
New York, New York 10036-8099
(212) 642-2946

■ Urban Survival Skills

The Yukon/Koyukuk Urban Survival Skills Program

The Yukon/Koyukuk School District has developed a checklist of urban survival skills that rural students need to learn. The checklist is kept on file for the students' entire high-school program. The Urban Survival program is incorporated into the vocational education's Print Shop program. In the print shop, students from 11 rural high schools travel into the district headquarters and spend two days in a dormitory setting while attending classes and assisting in the day-to-day operations of the district's print shop. Emphasis is placed on expectations found in a work environment, willingness to learn new skills, and on developing an attitude of becoming life-long learners. Here is the first page of this checklist.

Other skills covered in the same format are

Household survival: learn how to

> clean
> prepare meals
> do laundry
> plan menus
> shop for groceries

Finance: learn how to

> fill out credit application
> buy on credit
> read monthly bank statements
> balance a checkbook
> open a savings account
> purchase certificates
> prepare a budget
> apply for and use credit cards
> determine interest rates
> apply for loan (car, home, personal)
> establish credit

Urban Survival Skills

Name: _____

School: _____

Teacher: _____

Date (year and semester): _____

Sessions attended

Transportation - learn how to:	ID	OD	PS	AC	H	Cert. by
Use a bus						
Use a bus schedule						
Read a city map						
Obtain a driver's license						
Drive in a city						
Walk in a city safely						
Purchase a new/used car						
Obtain car insurance						
Use a travel agency						
Compare oil/gas prices						
Compare car repair costs						
Know what to do if involved in a car accident						
Maintain a car (used/new)						
Rent a car						
Make airline reservations						
Housing - learn how to:						
Rent an apartment or house						
Obtain utility service						
Make a hotel reservation						
Obtain campus housing						
Obtain off-campus housing						
Know differences - buy/lease/rent						
Lettered, numbers and fractional drill bits						

ID = Introduction of skill
OD = Observed demonstration of skill
PS = Practicing skill (working knowledge)

AC = Has achieved competency in skill
H = Total hours
Cert. by = Instructor certification

Communications: learn how to

    use the telephone
    use phone book in emergency
    use phone book for addresses
    contact people for help
    use newspaper to place ads and shop for prices
    use the radio
    use public bulletin board
    get help when lost
    get help for emergency housing
    use crisis line

Employment: learn how to

look for jobs
write a resume
dress for job interview
behave at interview
fill out a job application

Personal: learn how to

order food from menu
calculate a tip
pay a tab
use acceptable table manners
deal with domestic violence
maintain physical and mental health
obtain legal advice
get help and guidance
offset boredom
find and use city recreational facilities and locations
recognize and know what to do if you think you have a
    communicable disease
make sound decisions concerning drugs and alcohol

Contact

Yukon/Koyukuk School District
Box 309
Nenana, Alaska 99760

ASSOCIATION FOR STRANDED RURAL ALASKANS IN ANCHORAGE

Because they are unprepared, young people from rural Alaska
can be victimized in a large urban city.

One 13-year-old Native girl came into Anchorage with her
school group. The group decided to go shopping in one of the
local malls. The teacher felt she had prepared them for all they
might encounter. Unfortunately, she had not! The young girl left
her friends to go to the bathroom. Upon entering the bathroom

she noticed an elderly woman. Paying her no attention, she promptly went into the stall and sat down. The woman waited a few moments, pushed the stall door open and stared without speaking for several minutes. The girl was so afraid, she couldn't think what to do, so she did nothing. The woman finally left. The experience was so traumatic that, according to her teacher, the girl wanted to return home immediately. Since that was not possible, she didn't leave the teacher's side after the incident.

The police were called in another incident because a young woman had been standing outside a store for several hours. The security guard of the mall came and asked her what she was doing. Her aunt had told her not to talk to strangers, so she refused to talk to him. He called the police, thinking there was something wrong with the girl. A female officer responded. She asked the girl, "May I see your identification?" The girl replied, "No." The officer heard "No, you can't see my identification" and that is what caused the problem. When the officer took the girl's arm to take her to the squad car and check on identification, the girl became very frightened that she would not connect with her aunt and would be lost.

This could have been avoided if the first stop the school group made was to the free Association for Stranded Rural Alaskans in Anchorage Student Urban Survival orientation. This group did come to ASRAA, but it was on the third day of their trip. The teacher said she felt she had covered everything. ASRAA staff explained that because of their experience with similar incidents, they might have been able to help.

In the Student Survival course, students are given incidents that have actually happened to students in Anchorage. Opportunities are presented to them to see what can make a person a walking target, to encounter actual situations before they happen, and to decide what they can do to protect themselves from harm. This program began because many students were victimized as a result of lacking basic knowledge of personal safety and urban survival.

ASRAA includes education on urban survival skills, social services, employment skills, and crime prevention. The Student Urban Survival/Personal Safety course is especially designed for adolescents coming to Anchorage for field trips or vacation.

The course covers the bus system, shoplifting, traffic lights, personal safety, encounters with strangers, and dressing for safety, as well as highlights of things to see in Anchorage.

If you cannot bring the students to Anchorage for this workshop, you can request that information and curriculum guides be mailed to your school. ASRAA will provide these materials at their cost to rural schools. The village program consists of three components:

1. *Student urban survival:* Students learn what is needed, where and why to get identification, how to apply for and interview for jobs, how to use banks, and how to buy food cost-effectively.

2. *Basic Personal Safety/Crime Prevention Program:* Students learn how to avoid becoming walking targets on city streets, how to handle aggressive people, how to use defensive voice, how to handle incidents that have happened to other students, and how to make decisions before these or similar incidents happen to them. This curriculum reduces the villager's chance of becoming a victim.

3. *Cultural awareness training:* Teachers and counselors learn about basic cultural differences in Alaska, including cross-cultural communication skills. This training includes interactive student activities to make students more culturally aware.

ASRAA provides pretest and post-test materials, lends safety films, and makes other culturally appropriate materials available.

Contact

Association for Stranded Rural Alaskans in Anchorage
101 E Ninth Avenue #10B
Anchorage, Alaska 99501

■ Student Exchange Programs

"It was the first time in my life I had to go out to be accepted for what I was and did, and not because of my family." So spoke a Sutherland High School student from Tittsford, New York, after returning from an exchange program which included hiking out of the Grand Canyon.

The feeling of accomplishment at having met a challenge is a common one for these exchange students. The nature of the challenge varies from school to school. For the student sent out from Seldovia's Susan B. English High School, the challenge may be getting a ticket to a Broadway show in New York City or floating down the Green River in Colorado. For the teenage visitor to Seldovia, the challenge is the Project Adventure camping trip, during which participants sleep in the snow and climb a mountain.

This student and faculty exchange program is organized through the Network of Complementary Schools, a nonprofit consortium of public and independent schools from across the United States and in Toronto, Canada. Students generally exchange for three to ten weeks, teachers for a week or two.

All participating schools must meet the requirement of offering a specialized experiential education program or an intensive academic focus to the students. Each program is evaluated when the school applies for admission, through both documentation of success and an on-site inspection by the network. In screening, the network also strives for wide diversity of programs, equal geographical representation, and balance between public and independent schools. Thus, if your school were accepted into the network, your students could be placed in a wide variety of programs, including a college preparatory program at St. Benedict's; a school run by monks in the heart of Newark; a large professional theater in Albany, New York; an intensive music instruction program at Interlochen,

Michigan; or in a four-week seminar at the Elgin Academy in Elgin, Illinois where they learn about politics Chicago style.

A second exchange program the network sponsors is called "Walkabout," which lasts for an entire semester and involves students moving to four different schools, each of which helps them face a preconceived challenge. The four challenges usually include both intellectual and social service programs.

The annual network membership fee for each school is $550. The cost per exchange student is usually only the price of transportation.

Contact

The Network of Complementary Schools, Inc.
79 Main Street
Dover, Massachusetts 02030
(508) 785-2240

■ **Outdoor Skills**

Project Adventure

A Seldovia high-school student was walking by a small lake in Anchorage when he saw a canoe capsize and dump five people into the cold waters. Without hesitating, the boy leaped into the lake to aid the floundering people. Although he could not save the woman, he was able to rescue the man and three young children—four people who might otherwise have died. He attributed his ability to act to his school's Project Adventure program, which had given him the confidence, training, and rapid decision-making skills crucial in the emergency he encountered.

Project Adventure is a nationwide program that prepares students for an outdoor adventure. Survival training for emergency situations in the wilderness is an integral part of the

MIKE MATHERS

program. The program consists of three parts: the "Ropes Course," academic instruction, and fall and winter camping trips.

The Ropes Course consists of a series of activities that use constructing ropes and cables to teach climbing, emergency decision making, and teamwork. This seems a bewildering combination of objectives. But consider some of the activities:

- *The Wall Mount.* A team must get each member over a 12-foot-high wall, including the problematic last person.

- *The Burma Bridge Walk.* The student traverses a precarious rope bridge straight out of the climactic scene of Indiana Jones and the Temple of Doom.

- *The Free Fall.* The student falls off a 40-foot log and depends upon his fellow students to catch him!

Of course, the students are secured by basic safety hook-ups, nevertheless, they learn how to take responsibility for one another. Project Adventure "develops leadership skills for all, not just for the natural leaders," notes the Susan B. English school principal. "It is designed to build cooperation and teamwork."

The academic portion of the course teaches outdoor survival skills (e.g., how to prepare for a camping trip, how to use ropes in the wilderness, how to hunt, how to find water) and environmental information tailored to the environment of the local area.

The students then apply their new knowledge and skills to survive the outdoor adventure which usually is an extended camping trip. In Seldovia, students camp one weekend in fall and one weekend in winter to get accustomed to sleeping in the snow before they tackle the four to five day winter camping trip. The culmination of the adventure is a roped climb up a nearby mountain. Later in the year, graduating seniors who completed Project Adventure again climb "Graduation Peak" on the morning of convocation to have their pictures taken in their caps and gowns.

How To

Project Adventure can be run as an extracurricular activity or it can be offered as part of the curriculum.

Contact

> Project Adventure
> Hal Neese
> Alaska State Facilitator
> Alaska State Department of Education
> P.O. Box F
> Juneau, Alaska 99811
> (907) 465-2841

Summer Programs

■ Health Careers

The Della Keats Summer Enrichment Program is conducted for 24 Alaska Native rural junior and senior high-school students who are pursuing careers in health. Students receive six weeks of intensive preparatory instruction in math, anatomy and physiology, chemistry, English, and study skills.

In addition to academic preparation, students receive a full orientation to the UAA campus. The orientation includes information on admissions, financial aid, and academic counseling. Students participate in career shadowing days at a local hospital or health clinic, spending two days with a health professional.

Included in the Della Keats Summer Enrichment Program is a personal growth component that addresses social and emotional issues. Students are selected on the basis of their GPA, depth of high-school course work (especially math and science), career choice, essay, and letters of recommendation.

The goal of the Della Keats Summer Enrichment Program is to provide a bridging program to assist rural students in transition from high school to an urban university setting.

Contact

Katherine A. Johnson, R.N., director
Alaska Native Health Career Program
Della Keats Summer Enrichment Program
University of Alaska Anchorage
3211 Providence Drive, Building K, Room 104A
Anchorage, Alaska 99508
(907) 786-4644

■ **College Preparation**

THE RURAL ALASKA HONORS INSTITUTE

An Alaska student, aware of his math deficiency, summoned up his courage and signed up for two tough math courses during his senior year. The confidence came from the Rural Alaska Honors Institute. Many students find RAHI a turning point in their lives.

If you have bright students who are interested in attending college, encourage them to apply for RAHI. RAHI provides the opportunity for rural Alaska Native high-school students to spend six weeks of the summer between their junior and senior year at the University of Alaska Fairbanks. The students live in a dormitory, supervised by an adult and by upperclassmen familiar with rural areas, and take courses from a combination of high-school faculty and college teachers. The courses are those that are essential for succeeding in college—mathematics, writing, library skills, and team research projects. The program

JIM KOWALSKY

features an Alaska Native Land Claims Settlement Act course and simulated college courses taught by professors in engineering, business administration, science, education, and resource management.

Some students will return early to RAHI as graduated high-school students to get a head start with eight weeks of freshman English and math for college credit.

Even after the six-week summer program is over, RAHI continues to offer assistance to its former participants. When filling out college applications, they can call the RAHI office for help. RAHI also attempts to place its college students as summer interns with Native corporations.

How To

1. If you have juniors or RAHI seniors who are college-bound and have a 3.0 or better grade-point average, you can help them enter RAHI. Do not hesitate because of costs: RAHI pays for travel, tuition, and room and board.

2. Keep your eye out for the application packet which is sent in fall to every district and every rural school.

3. Since RAHI can work with only about 40 students each summer, competition for acceptance into the program is high. RAHI director Jim Kowalsky suggests the students pay close attention to writing the application essays, which are used by RAHI to judge student motivation, and to nominators' recommendation.

Contact

Rural Alaska Honors Institute
University of Alaska Fairbanks
Fairbanks, Alaska 99775
(907) 474-6886
fax (907) 474-5624

Other Summer Programs for Academically Advanced Students

Center for the Advancement of Academically Talented
Youth (CTY)
The Johns Hopkins University
Charles and 34th Streets
Baltimore, Maryland 21218
(301) 338-8427

■ Fine Arts

A 17-year-old boy mounts the stage ladder with yellow gel in his hand. There are no windows in the theater for the sun to flood through to create the afternoon scene of the play. Still, it will be a sunny afternoon in act IV. Under the guidance of a lighting design instructor, he has just learned how to create the effect of sunlight himself.

These camps offer junior and senior high-school students an opportunity to study music, the visual arts, drama, and dance under the tutelage of professional artists.

Fine Arts camps are held on the Mt. Edgecumbe High School campus in Sitka and the University of Alaska campus in Fairbanks. Each program has a different emphasis. Limited scholarships are available.

TODD PARIS

Contact

The camps send materials to the schools each year. For information on specific programs and application materials, contact:

Sitka:

Program Director
Alaska Arts Southeast Fine Arts Institute
Box 2133
Sitka, Alaska 99835
(907) 747-8177

Fairbanks:

Director
UAF Summer Fine Arts Camp
Music Department
University of Alaska Fairbanks
Fairbanks, Alaska 99775
(907) 474-6837 or 474-7555

9

Social Programs

The Alaska Council on Prevention of Alcohol and Drug Abuse is a nonprofit corporation dedicated to reducing the incidence and prevalence of alcohol and drug abuse and their related problems.

The Alaska Council on Prevention of Alcohol and Drug Abuse is responsible for providing many different substance abuse prevention programs around the state and for helping educators, parents, and community members implement them. Examples are:

Education and Training

- *Here's Looking At You, 2000:* This drug education program provides up-to-date drug information and emphasizes saying "no." The K–12 curriculum features lessons and activities designed to reduce factors that put young people at greater risk for drug or alcohol involvement. The curriculum delivers current information on alcohol and other drugs, chemical dependency and the family, fetal alcohol syndrome, and AIDS; social skills training such as refusal skills, assertiveness training, and friend-making skills; and bonding activities designed to promote positive relationships with school, family, and social peers.

The curriculum is replete with "no use" messages, firmly establishing nonuse as the healthiest choice. It also provides opportunities for parent involvement through newsletters and extension activities. Kits with teacher's manuals are available. Each kit includes a training program for teachers and interested community members. Two- and three-day teacher training sessions are available.

- *Natural Helpers:* This program identifies adolescents trusted by their schoolmates and trains them to help their peers cope with mood swings, drug and alcohol abuse, and difficulties with friends, family, and school. The *Leader's Guide* shows you how to establish a program in your school. The Natural Helpers Program was designed to augment already existing support networks among teens. Young people tend to seek out peers for help with problems associated with friends, parents, school, suicide, and alcohol and other drugs. Through a survey process, youth who are viewed by their peers as natural helpers are identified and invited to a three-day training seminar. The purpose of this training is not to establish these youth as counselors, but to help them become more effective helpers. Participants review the components of an effective helping relationship: communication skills, problem-solving techniques, trust building, assessment, and referral skills. Participants are also cautioned to recognize their own personal limitations as helpers. This adaptable program has also been successfully implemented with adults and senior citizens.

The following three curricula were created by Canada's Four Worlds Development Project:

- *Walking with Grandfather:* Where self-esteem and an appreciation of moral and cultural values is low, alcohol and other drug abuse is high. In groups where life-enhancing, life-preserving values are strong and active in the culture, social decay and substance abuse tend to be relatively low. This curriculum features stories such as

"Walking with Grandfather" and "The Great Wolf and Little Mouse Sister," which teach values to Native children in culturally appropriate ways. It can be used in the upper elementary classroom as well as in homes and communities to draw Native children closer to a way of life that promotes the development of human potential.

- *Unity in Diversity: Promoting an Understanding and Appreciation of the Human Family:* The purpose of this comprehensive, multicultural education program for junior high school students is to promote an understanding of the similarities that human beings share, the role of cultural differences in shaping behavior and beliefs, and of the roots and dynamics of prejudice. Teaching and learning strategies that have been proven to be effective agents for developing tolerance and understanding are used, including guided discussions, role plays, cooperative learning, and collaborative problem solving.

- *The Sacred Tree:* The Sacred Tree is a curriculum designed to address alcohol and other drug abuse in Native communities. A holistic view using the medicine wheel is emphasized, asking that all aspects of the student—physical, mental, emotional, and spiritual—be educated, and that each person's volition (will) become engaged in the process of his or her own development. The curriculum challenges and empowers young people (high school and young adults) to undertake a journey into personal and community growth. Substance use is viewed as an obstacle in the path of this journey.

Contact

Alaska Council on Prevention of Alcohol and Drug Abuse
3333 Denali, Suite 201
Anchorage, Alaska 99503
(907) 349-6602 or (800) 478-PREV (outside of Anchorage)
fax (907) 349-4323

Suicide Prevention

Alaska has one of the highest rates of suicide in the nation. The most endangered group is the Native male population between the ages of 18 and 25.

Teachers and other school personnel concerned about suicide prevention need to focus on prevention, intervention, and counseling.

Prevention involves the early identification of deeply troubled students by implementing programs that teach school personnel and students to recognize the warning signs of suicidal thinking and behavior.

Intervention involves developing sound policies and procedures to ensure that deeply troubled students receive prompt, appropriate help. It also means doing the training necessary to ensure that all school personnel know these procedures.

If a suicide, a serious suicide attempt, or an unexpected tragedy occurs that affects the school community, school personnel and other involved agencies will know how to inform the student body, inform and manage the media, and work together to identify, help, and support those most affected.

Resources

Fairbanks Crisis Line can be the critical link between your community and the resources needed for suicide prevention. It is available statewide and accepts collect calls from anywhere in Alaska. Crisis Line offers workshops that provide resources addressing suicide prevention.

The Crisis Line

452-HELP

- 24-hour telephone crisis intervention service
- Answered by trained volunteers
- The only crisis intervention telephone help line in the Interior
- Certified member, American Association of Suicidology
- Collect calls accepted

Fairbanks Crisis Line
520 Fifth Avenue
Box 221
Fairbanks, Alaska 99701
(907) 451-8600

More suicide prevention information is available from:

Division of Mental Health and Developmental Disabilities
Box H-01
Juneau, Alaska 99811-0620
(907) 465-3370

- *Native corporations* often have mental health programs and professionals who will come to your school to present them.

- *Various school districts* within and outside Alaska have developed a variety of suicide prevention programs. Some include classes for students; all contain policies and procedures for school staff. These include:

Fairbanks North Star Borough School District Crisis Intervention Handbook. There is a reference copy in each school in the principal's office. Its purpose is to provide a working resource for the building principal for crisis intervention in his or her school. The handbook is generic in nature and provides the building administrator with a checklist that will allow him or her to be proactive rather than reactive in dealing with a crisis. Contact the Fairbanks North Star Borough, P.O. Box 1250, Fairbanks, Alaska 99709.

Los Angeles Unified School District Psychologists First Aid Handbook. Compendium of materials organized around various topics that require some form of crisis intervention work. The handbook is specifically designed for use by school personnel. Contact Barbara Price, Valley Psychological Services, 6520 New Castle Avenue, Reseda, California 91335.

Adolescent Suicide Prevention Program: A Guide for Schools and Communities. Fairfax County Public Schools, Department of Student Services and Special Education, 10310 Layton Hall Drive, Fairfax, VA 22030. (703) 691-2964. School and community program including teacher training, parental involvement, professional involvement, and student stress program.

Suicide Prevention Program for California Public Schools.
Publication Sales, California State Department of Education, Box 271, Sacramento, California 95802.

- *Good resources for classroom use:*

Joan, Polly. *The Living Alternative Handbook,* Human Sciences Press. A curriculum for middle and secondary school students dealing with ways to understand and cope with depressive and suicidal feelings. Curriculum and intervention methods are included. Order through bookstores.

Cohen, George. *A Program on Depression and Suicide for High School Students.* A program developed by the Interagency Task Force on Suicide with the support of the Mental Health Association of Westchester County. Discussion of intervention strategies and resource materials.

Contact

George Cohen
White Plains Schools
5 Homeside Lane
White Plains, New York 10601

Irvine Unified School District Stages Curriculum. Curriculum developed for middle and secondary school students designed to teach skills to manage stressful reactions to change. Excellent lessons based on student's experiences.

Contact

Irvine Unified School District
Guidance Projects Division
31-B W Yale Loop
Irvine, California 92714
(714) 552-4882

Director of Educational Services
Suicide and Crisis Center
2208 Swiss Street
Dallas, Texas 75203
(214) 824-7020
Various programs including five lessons for classroom use.

- *Good general resources on adolescent suicide prevention:*

    Barrett, Thomas C. *Youth in Crisis: Seeking Solutions to Self-Destructive Behavior.* Presents background information on youth suicide and offers practical suggestions for identification, intervention, prevention, and the development of school and community prevention models.

Contact

    Sopris West, Inc.
    1120 Delaware Avenue
    Longmont, Colorado 80501
    (303) 651-2829

    Johnson, S. W. and Maile, L. J. 1987. *Suicide and the Schools, A Handbook for Prevention, Intervention, and Rehabilitation.* Springfield, Illinois: Charles Thomas. A comprehensive handbook for the schools, including roles and responsibilities for school personnel, warning signs, crisis intervention, and helping attempters and survivors in a school setting.

    Adolescent Suicide: A Prevention Resource Guide for the Family and Community
    Bureau of Mental Health
    450 W State Street
    Boise, Idaho 83720
    (208) 334-5531

CHILD ABUSE AND NEGLECT: THE ROLE OF THE TEACHER

Identification and Reporting of Child Abuse or Neglect

Alaska Statute 47.17 states that teachers, school personnel, and school administrators are mandated to report suspected child abuse or neglect. Most Alaska school districts and schools have a written policy on reporting. Investigation of child maltreatment is usually handled by the Alaska Division of Family and Youth Services (DFYS). If DFYS cannot be reached, the Alaska State Troopers, local police or the Village Public Safety Officer can also take the information. Failure to report suspected maltreatment is a class B misdemeanor.

Reports can be made anonymously. A good-faith clause in the law protects the reporter from liability if the report is made in good faith and not for slanderous purposes. If possible, it is best to identify yourself as a teacher, but sometimes people have personal reasons for not being identified. Do not let fear stop you from making the report. Remember, the fear of telling is even more so for the child.

Common indicators of *physical abuse* may include unexplained burns, bites, bruises, broken bones; fear of a parent; protests or cries when it is time to go home; reports of an injury by an adult; or extreme aggressiveness or sadistic-type behaviors toward another children or animals.

Signs of severe *physical neglect* include children who beg or steal food or money from classmates, who are consistently left alone at young ages to care for even younger children, who lack needed medical or dental care, who are consistently dirty and have severe body odor, or who have parents with severe alcohol or drug problems.

Sexual abuse should be suspected in children who sexually act out on other children; who are seductive and sexual in manners and behaviors towards adults; who contract a venereal disease or become pregnant, especially under the age of twelve; who demonstrate bizarre, sophisticated, or unusual sexual knowledge or behavior; who have genital trauma, infection, and difficulty walking or sitting; or who experience extreme behavior changes, mood swings, or sudden drops in grades during the school year.

If you are not sure, ask for advice on what to do. You need not give your name. Call the DFYS office closest to you or call toll free (800) 478-4444.

When making a report, follow the reporting procedure laid out by your school principal. Often, a district will identify one person to make all reports, allowing teachers to keep their relationships to the children intact.

Remember, you are not an investigator, you are a teacher. Let the social workers or the troopers who are trained in investigating abuse and interviewing children do their jobs.

Disclosure

A teacher plays many roles and is often a person a child turns to when assistance or protection is needed. In other cases, there may come a slip or some indication in a child's words that he or she has experienced abuse. These words may sound like this:

"He is doing stuff. He bothers me."
"I have something to say but you have to promise not to tell."
"He told me not to tell. He does bad things."

It is important not to let these things pass. Often children drop information and words to test your reaction. Follow-up studies with sexually abused children tell us that the moment the child first "discloses" is an extremely important step in the healing journey of that child.

If a child tells you about abuse,

- Stay calm

- Focus on what the child is telling you, not on your own feelings of discomfort.

- Listen carefully and give the child room to talk, but do not press for details. Do not assume. If the child uses words you do not understand, clarify their meaning but use the child's words.

- Let the child know you believe them and that they did the right thing in telling.

- Let the child know what you are going to do with the information.

When a child discloses, it is important to follow through with the reporting procedure of your school. As soon as possible after the disclosure, write down exactly how the child told you. Oftentimes our memories become faulty in the days or weeks it sometimes takes for investigation. Having an accurate record ensures that you are correct, exact, and are not letting your emotions color the child's words.

What Can You Do in Your Classroom?

Oftentimes the most healing place for a child who has been abused or neglected is the classroom. Teachers are not therapists, but nonetheless a caring warm environment within the school can be therapeutic. Some ways to encourage a healing environment include:

- All children need to feel lovable and capable. *Build self-esteem* through positive messages and words, choices, positive beginnings and endings to the day.

- *Build social skills* by promoting a cooperative, caring environment. Teach all the children how to get along, how to solve problems, and how to care for each other.

- *Provide structure and a dependable consistent routine.* Make your classroom a safe place, free of hitting, shaming, belittling, and verbal abuse from all members of the class. Ask permission before touching children to give them a gentle way to regain control over what happens to their bodies.

- If applicable in your classroom, *offer health education including sexual abuse prevention education.* Health educators, school nurses, and counselors are good resources.

- For ideas of how you as a teacher can help children heal from the effects of abuse, check with your school counselor, district psychologist, health educators, mental health workers, or call members of the organization nearest your village that deals with the problems of family violence or child abuse. (See the listing at the end of this section.)

Women's Shelters, Domestic Violence Network Programs, and Child Abuse Prevention Programs

Contact the agency in your area for more information on child abuse reporting and identification or prevention and education programs.

PART III

SOURCES OF

INFORMATION

The following compilation of resources represent a sampling of some of the more popular listings available to the small or rural school educator. Many times a teacher does not have the time or money to buy programs, investigate new materials, or spend hours looking at free samples and books from districts, and suppliers. We hope that this list of resources will help in your quest for quality information and instructional materials.

■ **Classic Books on Small Rural Schools**

Ashmore, M. Cathrine. *Risks and Rewards of Entrepreneurship.* St. Paul, Minnesota: EMC Publishing, (800) 328-1452.

Blackburn, J., & Powell, W. 1976. *One At a Time All at Once: The Creative Teacher's Guide to Individualized Instruction Without Anarchy.* Glenview, Illinois: Scott, Foresman.

Findley, J., & Tonsmeire, J. (Eds.). 1989. *The Wisdom of Practice: Adapting Curriculum to Meet the Needs of Rural Students.* Juneau, Alaska: Department of Education, Alaska Staff Development Network.

Gjelten, Tom. 1978. *Schooling in Isolated Communities.* Portland, Maine: North Haven Project for Career Development.

Herbert, Belle. 1982. *Shandaa: In My Lifetime.* Edited by Bill Pfisterer, translated by Katherine Peter. Fairbanks, Alaska: Alaska Native Language Center.

Keizer, Garret. 1988. *No Place But Here: A Teacher's Vocation in a Rural Community.* New York: Viking Penguin

Kleinfeld, J. S., McDiarmid, G. W., & Hagstrom, D. 1985. *Alaska's Small Rural High Schools: Are They Working?* Fairbanks, Alaska: Institute of Social & Economic Research and Center for Cross-Cultural Studies.

McDiarmid, G. W., Kleinfeld, J. S., & Parrett, W. 1988. *The Inventive Mind: Portraits of Rural Alaska Teachers.* Fairbanks, Alaska: Institute of Social & Economic Research and Center for Cross-Cultural Studies.

Nachtigal, Paul. 1982. *Rural Education: In Search of a Better Way.* Boulder, Colorado: Westview Press.

Peddiwell, J. Abner. 1939. *The Saber-Tooth Curriculum.* McGraw-Hill Book Company, Inc.

Sher, Jonathan (Ed.). 1977. *Education in Rural America: A Reassessment of Conventional Wisdom.* Boulder, Colorado: Westview Press.

Vick, Ann (Ed.). 1983. *The Cama-i Book.* Garden City, New York: Anchor Books.

Wigginton, Eliot. 1985. *Sometimes a Shining Moment: The Foxfire Experience.* Garden City, New York: Anchor Press/Doubleday.

Wigginton, Eliot (Ed.). 1976. *I Wish I Could Give My Son a Wild Raccoon.* Anchor Books.

Wigginton, Eliot. 1975. *Moments: The Foxfire Experience.* Published by IDEAS, Magnolia Star Route, Nederland, Colorado 80466.

Wigginton, Eliot, & Bennett, Margie (Eds.). The ongoing Foxfire book series. Garden City, New York: Anchor Books, Anchor Press/Doubleday.

Wood, Pamela. 1975. *You and Aunt Arie: A Guide to Cultural Journalism* based on Foxfire and its descendants. Lakewood, Colorado: Great America Printing Co.

Young, Timothy W. 1990. *Public Alternative Education: Options and Choice for Today's Schools.* New York: Teachers College Press.

■ Clearinghouses and Organizations Concerned with Small Schools

The Department of Education

The Department of Education (DOE) publishes a useful newspaper, *Alaska Education News,* and an indispensable directory of schools, educational institutions, and services in Alaska. DOE has published model curriculum guides for secondary school subjects. DOE staff include specialists in curriculum, vocational education, bilingual education, high technology, and other areas relevant to small schools. If you call for help, you are likely to get switched around to various people but you will probably find someone who knows the field and can connect you to the right networks.

Contact

> Alaska Department of Education
> P. O. Box F
> Juneau, Alaska 99811
> (907) 465-2644

The Northwest Regional Educational Laboratory

The laboratory has provided useful consulting services to Alaska school districts and to the Alaska Department of Education for many years. Their areas of expertise include effective schooling practices, evaluation methods for state and federal programs, sex equity, and reading and language development. Write for their product catalog.

Contact

> Northwest Regional Educational Laboratory
> 300 SW Sixth Avenue
> Portland, Oregon 97204
> (503) 275-9500

Educational Resources Information Center

The Educational Resources Information Center (ERIC) is a decentralized nationwide information system designed and supported by the U. S. Office of Education. It is designed to aid in the development of educational programs by disseminating research results, research-related materials, and other information of interest to educators. It publishes *Research in Education* (RIE), a monthly journal that abstracts ERIC report literature, and *Current Index to Journals in Education* (CIJE), a monthly journal that indexes and abstracts periodical literature. ERIC computer searches can be conducted on a wide variety of educational topics at minimal cost because of government financing.

Contact

> The Rasmuson Library at the University of Alaska Fairbanks maintains current ERIC records and documents and is an excellent resource for the educator.

> Educational Resources Information Center (ERIC)
> National Institute of Education
> Code 401
> Washington, D.C. 20202

The ERIC Clearinghouse on Rural Education, Small Schools, American Indians, Mexican-Americans, Migrants, Outdoor Education

The clearinghouse is the national repository for materials relating to small schools, rural education, and Native American education. They collect and disseminate everything from instructional materials to research reports. ERIC will also do computer searches on topics of your choice. Write or telephone them with a request and they will send you back document titles and abstracts from which you can order the entire documents. Write this clearinghouse and get yourself on their mailing list for news reports and fact sheets related to small schools.

Contact

> ERIC Clearinghouse on Rural Education, Small Schools, American Indians, Mexican-Americans, Migrants, Outdoor Education
> New Mexico State University
> Box 3AP
> Las Cruces, New Mexico 88003-0042
> (505) 646-2623

The National Information Center for Educational Media

The National Information Center for Educational Media (NICEM) is an independent information center and clearinghouse designed to collect, catalog, and disseminate information about all audiovisual materials distributed in this country. Provides printed indexes of various types of media and materials such as films, audiotapes, videotapes, transparencies, filmstrips, and records.

Contact

> National Information Center for Educational Media (NICEM)
> University of Southern California
> University Park
> Los Angeles, California 90007

The National Rural Development Institute

The National Rural Development Institute (NRDI) is a non-profit organization dedicated to the enhancement of rural and small school education. NRDI facilitates the exchange of resources and effective strategies through national conferences, research, publications, training, and related services.

> *The American Council on Rural Special Education* (ACRES) is a rural "community" at the national level, working to improve services to rural individuals with disabilities. ACRES members include special educators, direct service providers, administrators, teacher trainers, parents and others who are vitally concerned with the enhancement of services to rural individuals with disabilities.

> *National Rural and Small Schools Consortium* (NRSSC) is an action-oriented group of individuals and agencies working to enhance rural and small school education and to address associated problems. Over 30 national professional organizations are affiliated with the consortium.

> *Support services available to all interested parties:*
> - *Journal of Rural and Small Schools*
> - *Rural Special Education Quarterly*
> - bimonthly newsletters: *Classroom Clips, RuraLink*
> - Rural Resource Exchange Directories
> - Directory of Universities Preparing Rural School Personnel
> - Directory of Scholarships for Future Rural School Personnel

- Transition Strategies Manual
- Preservice Curriculum Modules
- In-service Modules
- Employment Incentives Manual
- Parent Resource Directory
- Reports of national research on a variety of topics
- Other publications addressing HIV education, practical strategies of serving at-risk students, personnel recruitment/retention, regional service delivery, special education delivery systems, teacher training, etc.
- electronic bulletin boards
- resource data banks

Contact

National Rural Development Institute
Western Washington University
Miller Hall 359
Bellingham, Washington 98225-9092
(206) 676-3576

Research for Better Schools

Research for Better Schools (RBS) is a private, non-profit educational firm founded in 1966. Its sponsors include many clients from the public and private sectors of the community. They support research and development projects that seek to improve educational practice. RBS is also funded by the U.S. Department of Education to serve as the regional educational laboratory of the mid-Atlantic region. In its capacity as a regional laboratory, RBS serves schools, school districts, educational and business associations, and organizations from New Jersey to the nation's capital. Linked to the other nine regional laboratories also funded by the department, RBS is part of a national network for educational improvement.

Contact

> Research for Better Schools
> 444 N Third Street
> Philadelphia, Pennsylvania 19123-4107
> (215) 574-9300

Rural Entrepreneurship through Action Learning

Rural Entrepreneurship through Action Learning (REAL) and its rural school-incubated enterprise program provide students with the opportunity to research, plan, set up and operate their own enterprises in cooperation with their local high school or community college. The program includes both a classroom component, in which students take entrepreneurship courses for academic credit, and an experiential component, in which students create and run "honest to goodness" ventures. The businesses developed have the potential to "graduate" with the students and to become independent enterprises. Participants learn not only the basics of doing business, but also a broad spectrum of thinking, communication, and technical skills.

Contact

> North Carolina REAL Enterprises
> 948 Old Post Road
> Chapel Hill, North Carolina 27514
> Phone (919) 929-3939
> fax (919) 942-3307

The National Coalition of Alternative Community Schools

The coalition has active groups in each state and publishes a directory of public and private alternative schools.

Contact

> National Coalition of Alternative Community Schools
> Ed Nagle, Chairman
> P.O. Box 2823
> Santa Fe, New Mexico 87504

Mary Ellen Bowen, Editor and Vice-Chairman
58 Schoolhouse Road
Summertown, Tennessee 38483

The International Affiliation of Alternative School Associations and Personnel

This group is dedicated to establishing and maintaining a communication network between alternative education associations via shared leadership, financial obligations, and responsibility of identified work tasks. Also, the affiliation will work toward assisting states and independent members to develop and maintain associations, alternative schools, programs, and services.

Contact

International Affiliation of Alternative School Associations
 and Personnel
Kathy Knudtson
1212 Seventh St. SE
Cedar Rapids, Iowa 52403

Institute for Responsive Education

Promotes equity in education, explores the variety of social and educational issues involved in providing quality education to all segments of American society. The institute publishes the journal *Equity and Choice.*

Contact

Institute for Responsive Education
605 Commonwealth Avenue
Boston, Massachusetts 02215

Cities-in-Schools, Inc.

Cities-in-Schools, Inc. brings public and private resources into schools to benefit at-risk students. It operates in 53 sites and maintains five regional offices.

Contact

> William Milliken, President
> 1023 15th Street NW, Suite 600
> Washington, D.C. 20005
> (202) 861-0230

City-As-School

City-as-School uses secondary schools to provide unique learning experiences in community sites. National Diffusion Network replications are located in 50 cities.

Contact

> Marie Reilly, Project Director
> 16 Clarkson Street
> New York, New York 10022
> (202) 645-6121

National Consortium on Alternatives for Youth at Risk, Inc.

The consortium deals mostly with alternatives for disrupted and adjudicated youth.

Contact

> National Consortium on Alternatives for Youth at Risk, Inc.
> 5250 17th Street, Suite 107
> Sarasota, Florida 34235
> (813) 378-4793

National Dropout Prevention Center

The National Dropout Prevention Center has established FOCUS, a resource network that can be tapped with a modem.

Contact

> Jay Smink, Executive Director
> Clemson University
> Clemson, South Carolina 29634-5111
> (803) 656-2599

National Dropout Prevention Network

This network has contacts in all states. It publishes a newsletter and also sponsors an annual conference.

Contact

National Dropout Prevention Network
P. O. Box 4067
Napa, California 94558
(707) 253-0821

National Society for Internships and Experiential Education

This society provides information on learning outside of the school setting.

Contact

Sally Migliore, Project Director
3509 Haworth Drive, Suite 207
Raleigh, North Carolina 27609
(919) 787-3263

■ **Rural and Small School Journals and Publications**

National Rural and Small Schools Consortium, *Journal of Rural and Small Schools*

The *Journal of Rural and Small Schools* is the official publication of the National Rural and Small Schools Consortium. It is the only national scholarly journal devoted exclusively to rural and small school education issues. The journal's purpose is to provide practical, field-oriented articles relevant to rural and small school district management and instruction.

Contact

Teri A. Lipinski, Ph.D., *JRSS* Editor
National Rural Development Institute
Miller Hall 359
Western Washington University
Bellingham, Washington 98225
(206) 676-3576

American Council on Rural Special Education, *Rural Special Education Quarterly*

The *Rural Special Education Quarterly* is produced by the National Rural Development Institute and the American Council on Rural Special Education. The quarterly is the only national scholarly publication solely devoted to rural special education issues. The purpose of the quarterly is to provide articles concerning federal and other events relevant to rural individuals with disabilities, progressive service delivery systems, reviews of relevant conferences and publications, and resources for rural special educators.

Contact

Editor
National Rural development Institute
Miller Hall 359
Western Washington University
Bellingham, Washington 98225
(206) 676-3576

The Rural Educator

The Rural Educator is a professional journal written for and by those involved in rural education and university faculty specializing in the area of rural development. It is intended to serve as a means of furthering communication between university faculty and rural educators in our public schools. It is also designed to provide up-to-date information in the area of rural education.

Contact

>Richard I. Fisher, Executive Editor
>*The Rural Educator*
>School of Occupational and Educational Studies
>Humanities Building
>Colorado State University
>Fort Collins, Colorado 80523

Journal of Rural Studies

The *Journal of Rural Studies* publishes research articles relating to such rural issues as society, demography, housing, employment, transport, services, land-use, recreation, agriculture, and conservation. The focus is on those areas encompassing extensive land-use, with small-scale and diffuse settlement patterns and communities linked into surrounding landscape and milieux. Particular emphasis will be given to aspects of planning policy and management. The *journal* is international and interdisciplinary in scope and content.

Contact

>Pergamon Journals Inc.
>Maxwell House
>Fairview Park
>Elmsford, New York 10523
>(914) 592-7700

Equity and Choice

Equity and Choice is devoted to providing a forum for the exchange of ideas, insights, and practices among those working to increase educational equity. Its contents include analyses of new issues facing equity constituencies, summaries of research evidence that has practical import, in-depth case studies of successful projects, and descriptions of useful resources.

Contact

>Institute for Responsive Education
>605 Commonwealth Avenue
>Boston, Massachusetts 02215
>(617) 353-3309

Fine Print

An occasional newsletter focusing on extraordinary institutional practices, remarkable schools, and commentary on various national and state strategies for the reform of education.

Contact

Joe Nathan, Editor
Humphrey Institute
University of Minnesota
301 19th Avenue S
Minneapolis, Minnesota 55455
(612) 625-3506

Center for Cross-Cultural Studies, University of Alaska Fairbanks

The Center for Cross-Cultural Studies (CXCS) is the research and development unit of the University of Alaska Fairbanks' College of Rural Alaska. The center is responsible for conducting applied research and development projects addressing the unique educational issues and problems inherent in Alaska's multicultural population. CXCS issues publications and reports to improve cross-cultural understanding.

Allen, Arthur W., III. 1990. *Cross-Cultural Counseling: The Guidance Project and the Reluctant Seniors.*

Anonymous. 1989. *A Student Teacher's Troubled Teaching Experience in Rural Alaska.*

Anonymous. 1988. *The Teacher Who Came to Rivertown: A Case Study.*

Barnhardt, Carol. 1985. *Historical Status of Elementary Schools in Rural Alaskan Communities, 1867-1980.*

Barnhardt, Ray (Ed.). 1977. *Cross-Cultural Issues in Alaskan Education,* Volume 1.

Barnhardt, Ray (Ed.). 1982. *Cross-Cultural Issues in Alaskan Education,* Volume 2.

Barnhardt, Ray. 1981. *Culture, Community, and the Curriculum.*

Barnhardt, Ray (Ed.). 1979. *Small High School Programs for Rural Alaska.*

Curriculum Resources for the Alaskan Environment: Energy Options. A Curriculum Guide. University of Alaska Fairbanks. 1980. 47pp.

Diamondstone, Judy & Barnhardt, Ray. 1990. *Curriculum Resources for the Alaskan Environment*.

Finley, Paris. 1990. *Gender Wars at John Adams High School: A Case Study*.

Finley, Paris. 1988. *Malaise of the Spirit: A Case Study*.

Forbes, Norma. 1984. *Television's Effects on Rural Alaska: Summary of Final Report*.

Getches, David. 1977. *Law and Alaska Native Education*.

Getches, Daivd. 1976. *A Primer on Laws Important to Alaska Native Education*.

Gumm, Richard. 1983. *Curriculum Resources for the Alaskan Environment: Review of Secondary Level ANCSA Educational Materials*.

Harrison, Barbara. 1985. *Manokotak: A Case Study of Rural School Development in Alaska*.

Kleinfeld, Judith (Ed.). 1989. *Cross-Cultural Teaching Tales*.

Kleinfeld, Judith. 1973. *A Long Way from Home*.

Kleinfeld, Gorusch, Kerr. 1988. *Minorities in Higher Education: The Changing North*.

McDiarmid, G., & Kleinfeld, J. 1982. ... *Doctor, Lawyer, Indian Chief: The Educational and Occupational Aspirations, Plans, and Preferences of Eskimo Students on the Lower Yukon*.

McDiarmid, G.Williamson. 1981. *Getting It Together in Chevak: A Case Study of a Youth Organization in a Rural Alaskan Village*.

Napoleon, Harold. 1991. *Yuuyaraq: The Way of the Human Being*. Edited by Eric Madsen.

Parrett, Orvik, Stephens. 1984. *The McKinley School Project*.

Salzman, Michael. 1991. *A Navajo Intercultural Sensitizer*.

Sponder, Barry. 1991. *Distance Education in Rural Alaska*.

Steiger, Neil. 1991. *On a White Horse: A Case Study*.

Photocopies Available:

Dauenhauer, Richard L. 1981. *Conflicting Visions in Alaskan Education.*

Harrison, Barbara. 1981. *Informal Learning Among Yup'ik Eskimos: An Ethnographic Study of One Alaskan Village.*

Kleinfeld, Judith. 1979. *Eskimo School on the Andreafsky: A Study of Effective Bicultural Education.*

McBeath, Gerald. 1983. *Rural Teachers and Community Schools in Alaska.*

McBeath, Kleinfeld, McDiarmid. 1983. *Patterns of Control in Rural Alaska Education.*

Scollon, Ron. 1981. *Human Knowledge and the Institution's Knowledge: Communication Patterns and Retention in a Public University.*

Contact

Resource Center
Center for Cross-Cultural Studies
University of Alaska Fairbanks
7th Floor Gruening
Fairbanks, Alaska 99775
(907) 474-6474

Other Publications

Contacts

Changing Schools
Mary Ellen Sweeney, Editor
98 N Wadsworth Boulevard #127
Lakewood, Colorado 82226
(303) 458-4313

Foxfire Magazine
Foxfire Fund, Inc.
Rabun Gap, Georgia 30568
Published quarterly by the students of the Rabun County
High School in Clayton, Georgia

■ Autobiographies in the Yukon-Koyukuk School District of Alaska Series

This is a series of autobiographies of people who live in some of the villages served by the Yukon-Koyukuk School District. The books are designed for upper level elementary students living in rural Alaska. Their appeal, however, is much wider. They may interest readers of any age.

The series tells stories of the rich and varied, though often neglected, Native cultures of interior Alaska. The books invite Alaska students to look closer to home and to examine change that has taken place in a historically short time. For students outside of Alaska, the books provide a view of a time and a place they would otherwise probably never encounter.

Curt Madison and Yvonne Yarber are first listed as writers for numbers 1–6 and later as interviewers and editors beginning with number 7. Hancock House Publishers Ltd. of North Vancouver, B. C., are the publishers of numbers 1–9 and Spirit Mountain Press of Fairbanks, Alaska, published numbers 10–21.

1. Moses Henzie. Allakaket. 1979.
2. Oscar Nictune, Sr. Alatna. 1980
3. Henry Beatus, Sr. Hughes. 1980.
4. Frank Tobuk. Evansville. 1980.
5. Joe Beetus. Hughes. 1980.
6. Madeline Solomon. Koyukuk. 1981.
7. Roger Dayton. Koyukuk. 1981.
8. Edwin Simon. Huslia. 1981.
9. John Honea. Ruby. 1981.
10. Edgar Kallands. Kaltag. 1982
11. Josephine Roberts. Tanana. 1983.
12. Billy McCarty, Sr. Ruby. 1983.
13. Simeon Mountain. Nulato. 1983.
14. Altona Brown. Ruby. 1983.
15. Chuck and Gladys Dart. Manley. 1984.
16. Goodwin Semaken. Kaltag. 1984.
17. Henry Ekada. Nulato. 1986.
18. Stanley Dayo. Manley. 1986.
19. Peter John. Minto. 1986.
20. Al Wright. Minto. 1986.
21. Martha Joe. Nulato. 1987.

Contact

Yukon/Koyukuk School District
Box 309
Nenana, Alaska 99760
(907) 832-5594.

■ Global Education Resources

B.C. Global Education Project
B.C. Teacher's Federation
2235 Burrard Street
Vancouver, British Columbia V6J 3H9
Canada

California International Studies Project (CISP)
Center for Research in International Studies/
Stanford Program on International and Cross-Cultural
   Education (SPICE)
Lou Henry Hoover Building, #200
Stanford University
Stanford, California 94305-2319
(415) 497-1114

The Canadian Institute for International Peace & Security
Suite 900, 3600 Albert Street
Ottawa, Ontario K1R 7H7
Canada
(613) 990-1593
fax (613) 563-0894

Canadian Peace Educators' Network
c/o The Pembina Institute
P. O. Box 839
Drayton Valley, Alberta T0E 0M0
Canada

Center for Teaching International Relations
University of Denver
University Park
Denver, Colorado 80208
(303) 871-3106

Experiment in International Living
19 Cedar Street
Brattleboro, Vermont 05301
(802) 254-4439

Foreign Policy Association
729 Seventh Avenue
New York, New York 10019
(212) 764-4050

Foreign Policy Association, Director
Department of School Programs
1800 M Street, NW
Washington, D.C. 20036
(202) 293-0046

Global Alliance for Tranforming Education (GATE)
4202 Ashwoody Trail
Atlanta, Georgia 30319
(404) 458-5678
fax (404) 454-9749

Global Awareness Program
College of Education
Florida International University
Tamiami Trail
Miami, Florida 33199
(305) 554-2664

Global Education Associates
475 Riverside Drive, Suite 456
New York, New York 10115

Global Education Center (GEC)
110 Pattee Hall
150 Pillsbury Drive, SE
University of Minnesota
Minneapolis, Minnesota 55455
(612) 624-0584 or 624-0555

Global Education Outreach
1511 K Street, NW, Suite 842
Washington, D.C. 20005
(202) 783-1156

Global Educators
P.O. Box 9976
Mills College
Oakland, California 94613
(415) 430-9976

Global Learning, Inc.
40 S Fullerton Avenue
Montclair, New Jersey 07042
(201) 783-7616

International Education Consortium
6800 Wydown Boulevard
St. Louis, Missouri 63105

International Studies Association
James F. Byrnes International Center
University of South Carolina
Columbia, South Carolina 29208

Massachusetts Global Education Project
18 Franklin Street
Belmont, Massachusetts 02178
(617) 712-7020

Mershon Center
Citizenship Development & Global Education Program
199 W Tenth Avenue
Columbus, Ohio 43201
(614) 292-1681

Victoria International Development Education Association
(VIDEA)
407-620 View Street
Victoria, British Columbia V8W 1J6
Canada
(604) 385-2333

■ Commercial Resources

The Learning Store

This store specializes in early childhood through high school materials.

Contact

Delores Doogan
The Learning Store
107 S. Seward Street
Juneau, Alaska 99801
(907) 586-5700

Scavengers Science Education Supply Company

This privately-owned company has a mail order catalog of materials that includes the areas of science, natural history, and cross-cultural education with an emphasis on the Alaska and northern environment. The company will mail a catalog upon request.

Contact

Scavengers Science Supply Co.
P.O. Box 211328
Auke Bay, Alaska 99821
(907) 789-1375

Schoolhouse Express, Inc.

This company provides early childhood and elementary materials. Call for a free catalog.

Contact

> Schoolhouse Express, Inc.
> 246 Illinois Street
> Fairbanks, Alaska 99701
> (907) 456-8262 *or*
> (800) 478-8262

The Teachers Store

This store provides comprehensive educational resources for the Alaska educator. Special emphasis is put on providing whole language across the curriculum units and activities for educators in rural Alaska settings.

Contact

> Jane Niebergal
> Mariswood Educational Resources
> The Teachers Store
> 1057 W 32nd Avenue
> P. O. Box 221955
> Anchorage, Alaska 99522
> (907) 277-7323